Measuring Risk Aversion

Measuring Risk Aversion

Donald J. Meyer

*Western Michigan University
Department of Economics
Kalamazoo, MI 49008, USA*

donald.meyer@wmich.edu

Jack Meyer

*Michigan State University
Department of Economics
East Lansing, MI 48824, USA*

jmeyer@msu.edu

Boston – Delft

Foundations and Trends® in Microeconomics

Published, sold and distributed by:
now Publishers Inc.
PO Box 1024
Hanover, MA 02339
USA
Tel. +1-781-985-4510
www.nowpublishers.com
sales@nowpublishers.com

Outside North America:
now Publishers Inc.
PO Box 179
2600 AD Delft
The Netherlands
Tel. +31-6-51115274

A Cataloging-in-Publication record is available from the Library of Congress

The preferred citation for this publication is D.J. Meyer and J. Meyer, Measuring Risk Aversion, Foundation and Trends® in Microeconomics, vol 2, no 2, pp 107–203, 2006

Printed on acid-free paper

ISBN: 1-933019-45-X
© 2006 D.J. Meyer and J. Meyer

Editorial Scope

Foundations and Trends® in Microeconomics will publish survey and tutorial articles in the following topics:

- Environmental Economics
- Contingent Valuation
- Environmental Health Risks
- Climate Change
- Endangered Species
- Market-based Policy Instruments
- Health Economics
- Moral Hazard
- Medical Care Markets
- Medical Malpractice
- Insurance economics
- Industrial Organization
- Theory of the Firm
- Regulatory Economics
- Market Structure
- Auctions
- Monopolies and Antitrust
- Transaction Cost Economics
- Labor Economics
- Labor Supply
- Labor Demand
- Labor Market Institutions
- Search Theory
- Wage Structure
- Income Distribution
- Race and Gender
- Law and Economics
- Models of Litigation
- Crime
- Torts, Contracts and Property
- Constitutional Law
- Public Economics
- Public Goods
- Environmental Taxation
- Social Insurance
- Public Finance
- International Taxation

Information for Librarians

Foundations and Trends® in Microeconomics, 2006, Volume 2, 4 issues. ISSN paper version 1547-9846. ISSN online version 1547-9854. Also available as a combined paper and online subscription.

Foundations and Trends® in
Microeconomics
Vol. 2, No 2 (2006) 107–203
© 2006 D.J. Meyer and J. Meyer
DOI: 10.1561/0700000006

Measuring Risk Aversion

Donald J. Meyer[1] and Jack Meyer[2]

[1] Western Michigan University, Department of Economics, Kalamazoo, MI 49008, USA, donald.meyer@wmich.edu
[2] Michigan State University, Department of Economics, East Lansing, MI 48824, USA, jmeyer@msu.edu

Abstract

The purpose of the survey is to summarize, discuss, and interpret published research concerning the risk aversion of decision makers who maximize expected utility. In doing this, two points are emphasized. First, any measure of risk aversion is specific to the particular outcome variable over which the measure is defined or estimated, and second when outcome variables are related, then their risk aversion measures are also related. These two points are used to show that a substantial portion of the reported variation in magnitudes and slopes of risk aversion measures from the research of the past forty years results from differences in the outcome variables, and when these differences are adjusted for, those findings are a quite consistent body of evidence.

Contents

1

Introduction

The measurement of a decision maker's propensity to accept or reject risk is an important and well researched topic. The purpose of this survey is to summarize, discuss, and interpret published research on this topic for decision makers who maximize expected utility. Expected utility was made a prominent tool of economic analysis in the 1940s by Von Neumann and Morgenstern (1944). Risk aversion and the size and nature of a decision maker's reaction to risk was extensively discussed by Friedman and Savage (1948, 1952). It was not until the work of Arrow (1965, 1971) and Pratt (1964), who define measures of risk aversion, however, that the quantification of the propensity to take risks for *single dimension* outcome variables could begin.[1] The focus in this review is on the information that has been provided concerning the Arrow-Pratt measure of relative risk aversion, although absolute risk

---

[1] The work presented here focuses on utility functions with outcomes that are of a single dimension. When more than one component is used to describe the outcome, such as the level of consumption in two time periods, or both the measure of health and wealth of the decision maker, then measuring the propensity to take risk becomes a more complicated matter. Except for a very brief mention in Section 4 when discussing consumption, this aspect of risk aversion is not discussed here.

aversion, partial risk aversion, risk tolerance and other measures are also briefly discussed.

More than forty years have passed since measures of risk aversion were first defined by Arrow (1965, 1971) and by Pratt (1964). During these years theoretical analysis has presented a large number of theorems that use assumptions concerning the level and slope of risk aversion in order to predict choices made by decision makers. These predictions are then compared with the observed decisions. When the predicted decisions match those that are observed, the assumptions leading to the predictions are supported, and when the predictions are the opposite of what is observed, the assumptions are rejected. In this way certain properties of the various risk aversion measures, such as decreasing absolute risk aversion for wealth, have become well accepted, while other properties such as increasing absolute risk aversion for wealth have been rejected.

During this same forty year time period, various empirical studies have attempted to directly determine which levels and slopes for risk aversion are consistent with the observed choices of a variety of decision makers. The evidence provided from this analysis has varied widely, and presents seemingly contradictory results concerning the slope and magnitude of risk aversion. Examining, interpreting and consolidating this evidence, and comparing it with the findings obtained in theoretical analysis is one of the main tasks of this work.

The risk taking propensity of a number of different groups of decision makers has been studied. Included are investors who allocate wealth among assets, consumers who choose consumption levels across time, agricultural producers who make various choices so as to maximize expected utility from net income or profit, and other such groups. Within each of these groups of decision makers, the particular decisions examined are also quite varied. As a result, each study selects an outcome variable that is consistent with the purposes of the study, and it is often the case that this outcome variable is not identical to that chosen by another. Hence a large number of different outcome variables have been employed in the discussion of the risk aversion of decision makers. These outcome variables include wealth, income, consumption, return, rate of return, net income, payoff and profit.

In addition to a variety of differently named outcome variables, in many instances different definitions or measures are employed for a particular outcome variable even though the name used remains the same. This makes the number of different outcome variables that have been examined even larger. For instance, one study of portfolio choice may use wealth as the outcome variable and in that study the taxation of investment income is ignored. Another study examines exactly the same decision, and considers the outcome variable to be final wealth, but explicitly models the taxation of investment gains. Even though the outcome variable is referred to as wealth in each of the studies, in the one case this variable is before-tax wealth, and in the other it is wealth after taxes are paid on investment income. Such differences in the way an outcome variable is defined or measured, even though they seem to be minor, can lead to significantly different estimates of the risk aversion measure, or require that different conditions be imposed on that measure.

When outcome variables differ, but are related to one another in a known way, the relationship between the outcome variables determines the relationship between their risk aversion measures. In many cases the relationship between outcome variables is implied by their definitions, and the definitions themselves can be used to indicate how the risk aversion measures are related to one another. Such is the case for the wealth and after-tax wealth outcome variables that were just mentioned.

Similar variation in outcome variables occurs in empirical analysis. Different measures are used for an outcome variable in the various studies. In one study, the wealth attributed to a decision maker making portfolio or other choices may include the value of owned housing, the value of life insurance, or the value of human capital, while another study may exclude these components when measuring wealth. Data availability sometimes determines what is included and what is excluded when measuring a particular outcome variable. This variation in the way the outcome variable is measured leads to predictable differences in the estimated magnitudes and slopes for risk aversion that are obtained. Once the variation is recognized, adjustments can be made so that the results are more easily compared across studies.

This variation in the outcome variables has led to different estimates of, and conditions imposed on, the slope and magnitude of risk aversion measures. It is important to recognize that for each of the studies, theoretical or empirical, the reported information directly pertains only to the risk taking propensity for the particular outcome variable examined. Furthermore, this information cannot usually be used to make statements concerning the risk taking propensity for other outcome variables without making adjustments. The literature is filled with examples where this point has been ignored, and the evidence from one study has been inappropriately used as information concerning risk aversion for a different outcome variable. Many studies publish tables which list the estimated values for relative risk aversion for different outcome variables when those values are not comparable. Great care must be exercised in using the findings concerning the magnitude and slope of risk aversion presented in any particular analysis.

The fundamental point made in the analysis here is that even though information concerning risk aversion in a particular study is always for the specific outcome variable employed in that study, the manner in which the various outcome variables are related to one another determines how their respective risk aversion measures are related. Thus, information concerning the relationship between outcome variables can be used to adjust the risk aversion information obtained for the one, so that this same information also applies to another. One of the contributions of this study is a detailed discussion of how to go about the task of making such adjustments.

This adjustment of risk preference information so that the various separate bodies of information can be more easily compared also allows one to consolidate the wide array of information concerning risk aversion. An important step in this process is to choose one outcome variable to which all others can be related and compared, a reference outcome variable. Wealth, as the term is used by Arrow (1965, 1971) and Pratt (1964), is selected as this reference outcome variable, and an attempt is made to relate all other outcome variables to Arrow-Pratt (A-P) wealth. Doing this allows the reported information on risk aversion for other outcome variables to be appropriately adjusted so that each of the studies provides information concerning risk aversion for

(A-P) wealth. By adjusting all information to this common scale, results across studies can be more easily summarized and directly compared, and the body of information concerning risk aversion can be examined as a whole rather than as individual parts.

Casual inspection of the findings concerning the magnitude and slope of risk aversion obtained during the past forty years indicates that both the magnitude and the slope of risk aversion varies widely across groups of decision makers, and even varies with the decisions that are made. Estimates of the magnitude of relative risk aversion range widely from near zero to values approaching one hundred, and whether the slope of the risk aversion measure is positive, negative or zero is an unsettled question for many measures, including relative risk aversion. The review here attempts to show that a substantial part of this variation is due to the differences in the outcome variables used in the analysis. After adjusting and consolidating the information, the situation is quite different. Evidence concerning the risk taking characteristics of representative decision makers of various types, making a variety of decisions, is quite consistent. Representative farmers choosing production strategies, representative investors choosing portfolio composition, and representative consumers optimally deciding on consumption over time are quite similar in their propensities to accept risk.

2

The Framework

2.1 Functions used to represent the propensity to take risks

There are many different functions that can be and are used to identify or represent the risk preferences of a particular decision maker who maximizes expected utility from outcome variable W. Each of these functions has its own particular uses, and each method of representing risk preferences has advantages and disadvantages. Several of these representation functions are described here, and their uses, advantages, and disadvantages are mentioned. One function, the measure of relative risk aversion, is selected as the primary function discussed in this review, and the reasons for its selection are given.

When the function representing the risk taking propensity of the expected utility maximizing decision maker is to be used to determine the decision maker's choice from a particular set of alternatives, $u(W)$, the von-Neumann-Morgenstern (N-M) utility function itself, is the most convenient representation of the person's risk preferences to have available. With this function, one simply searches among the available alternatives for the one that yields the largest expected value for the utility function. Of course, N-M utility functions are formulated for exactly this purpose. The reason this point is mentioned is that for any other function representing risk preferences, it is an advantage when that function can be transformed into the utility function. That is, the alternate representation should completely describe the risk preferences of the decision maker, and when it can be transformed into the N-M utility function, this is the case.

The primary disadvantage of using the utility function to represent a decision maker's propensity to accept risks, and one reason why other functions have been proposed, is that the N-M utility function is only unique to a positive linear transformation; that is, if $u(W)$ represents the risk taking propensity of a particular decision maker, then so does $a + b \cdot u(W)$ for any value for a, and any positive value for b. Thus, even though an N-M utility function completely describes risk preferences, it does not do so uniquely. It is this lack of uniqueness that implies that comparing risk preferences across decision makers using simple features such as the utility function's magnitude, slope or elasticity is quite meaningless for N-M utility functions.

The first two derivatives of $u(W)$ are also sometimes used to represent the risk taking propensity of the decision maker. Taking the derivative of $u(W)$, once or more than once, eliminates one of the two arbitrary parameters which make the N-M utility function not a unique representation, but not both. The derived function is still not unique, it is now unique only up to an arbitrary positive scale factor. For instance, if $u'(W)$ represents a particular decision maker by giving the decision maker's marginal utility, then so does $b \cdot u'(W)$ for any positive value for b. The same is true for all higher order derivatives of the utility function.

Marginal utility is often a useful way to represent the decision maker's risk preferences, especially when comparative statics is a primary consideration, or when the value for a parameter that can be continuously varied is being selected. When the decision being made involves choosing a value for a variable that can be continuously adjusted, most theoretical analysis of such decisions are formulated in such a way that the expected utility maximizing value for the choice variable is identified as the solution to a first order equation which involves the marginal utility function rather than the utility function itself. For example, when choosing the proportion of wealth to allocate to a risky and riskless asset, the optimal quantity can be determined as the solution to a first order equation. In this first order equation, the risk preferences of the decision maker are represented by the decision maker's marginal utility function.

Marginal utility does allow the utility function to be recovered as long as marginal utility is integrable. When $u'(W)$ is known, integration of $u'(W)$ yields $u(W)$ except for an arbitrary additive constant. Of course, for some marginal utility functions, the integration may not be able to be carried out.[2] The utility function that is obtained by integrating marginal utility is not unique for two reasons. First, there is the arbitrary scaling factor associated with the marginal utility function itself, and second, integration introduces an arbitrary additive constant of integration. Thus, when utility is obtained from marginal utility the exact same arbitrary parameters are associated with the utility function that is obtained.

As indicated earlier, the second derivative of $u(W)$, $u''(W)$, is also only unique to an arbitrary positive scale factor. Combining this with the fact that $u''(W)$ is not sufficient to allow one to recover $u(W)$ by using integration, makes $u''(W)$ a less than desirable choice as a function for representing risk preferences. The same $u''(W)$ represents more than one set of risk preferences, and furthermore it is not even a unique representation of those preferences. The slope of marginal utility, $u''(W)$, does have one advantage. It is one way to measure the curvature of $u(W)$, and this curvature is known to be related to the decision maker's propensity to accept risks. Arrow (1965, 1971) and Pratt (1964) make this point and present two other functions which are referred to as measures of risk aversion. These functions take

---

[2] Meyer and Meyer (2005a) use marginal utility to identify the risk taking propensity of a decision maker in a setting where only the first order conditions for an optimization model are being tested. Thus, the utility function itself is not needed to carry out the analysis. They use a particular marginal utility function for which the utility function itself is not of closed form, but involves incomplete gamma functions. Nonetheless, the risk preferences identified are simple, have convenient risk aversion measures and can be used for many purposes including the comparative static analysis carried out there. Roche (2005) provides additional details and an alternative to the utility function presented by Meyer and Meyer, and this alternative also displays decreasing relative risk aversion.

advantage of the positive feature of $u''(W)$, yet remove its disadvantages by appropriately combining $u''(W)$ with $u'(W)$.

These advantages and disadvantages of using utility or derivatives of utility to represent the risk taking propensities of decision makers led Arrow (1965, 1971) and Pratt (1964) to each define two other functions to describe the propensity to take risk. They refer to these functions as measures of risk aversion. Although far from being the only measures that could be defined, the two measures defined by Arrow (1965, 1971) and Pratt (1964) have become the standard terms used when discussing a decision maker's propensity to accept risk. The first measure, the measure of absolute risk aversion, $A(W)$, is defined by

$$A(W) = \frac{-u''(W)}{u'(W)}$$

This representation of the decision maker's risk preferences is unique. By taking the derivative of utility, the additive constant in the arbitrary positive linear transformation of utility is eliminated, and by forming the ratio of the two derivatives, the multiplicative constant is eliminated as well. Thus, all utility functions representing a particular decision maker's risk preferences result in exactly this same absolute risk aversion measure.

Although $A(W)$ is a unique representation of risk preferences, it is insufficient to completely describe those preferences. It is the case for instance that both $u(W)$ and $-u(W)$ have the same absolute risk aversion measure. Thus, when attempting to recover the utility function from an absolute risk aversion measure, an additional assumption is needed. The assumption commonly made in economics is that the utility function $u(W)$ is an increasing function. This assumption reflects the choice made by economists to focus on outcome variables for which larger values are always preferred to smaller values. With this monotonicity assumption, utility can be determined by carrying out the steps involved in the expression presented by Pratt (1964) and reproduced below. Of course, as with integrating marginal utility, actually carrying out the integration designated in these steps may be impossible.

$$u(W) = \int e^{-\int A(W)} \qquad (2.1)$$

Thus, absolute risk aversion uniquely describes a decision maker's propensity to accept risk, and does so completely, describing only one such decision maker as long as marginal utility is assumed to be positive. It is this feature of $A(W)$, that it is a complete and unique representation of risk preferences, that makes a comparison of the magnitude and slope of $A(W)$ across decision makers a potentially meaningful and useful exercise. $A(W)$ has been used extensively in describing the risk taking properties of expected utility maximizing decision makers, and estimates of its magnitude and slope have been made. Some of this information is reviewed in later sections.

Using absolute risk aversion, $A(W)$, to represent the risk preferences of a decision maker, however, has one particular disadvantage. The disadvantage involves the effect on $A(W)$ of scaling the outcome variable. Simply put, when the same outcome variable is quantified using a different unit of measure, the measure of absolute risk aversion associated with the utility function for that outcome variable is altered. In the literature reviewed, instances are encountered where different currencies are used to measure wealth, where wealth is measured nominally but at different points in time, or where rate of return is entered in decimal rather than percentage form. These variations in the unit of measure for the outcome variable alter the measure of absolute risk aversion that is obtained for that outcome variable.

To illustrate the effect of scaling, assume that W is scaled by factor t so that $X = t \cdot W$. X and W are the same outcome variable measured using two different units of measure. This relationship between X and W implies that the two utility functions $v(X)$ and $u(W)$, are related by $v(X) = v(t \cdot W) = u(W)$. Using this relationship, it is easily confirmed that

$$t \cdot A_v(X) = t \cdot \left(\frac{-v''(X)}{v'(X)} \right) = \frac{-u''(W)}{u'(W)} = A_u(W) \qquad (2.2)$$

Thus, the absolute risk aversion measure for utility function $u(W)$ is t times that for utility function $v(X)$. For instance, when W is rate of return in decimal form, and X is that same information expressed in percentage form so that $X = 100 \cdot W$, the decision maker's absolute risk aversion measures for these two outcome variables differ by a factor

of one hundred. This disadvantage of the absolute risk aversion measure
can easily be corrected for by making sure that the unit in which the
outcome variable is measured is consistent across the various studies
being compared. It is more convenient, however, to instead use a different function to represent the risk preferences of the decision maker.
This function, the relative risk aversion measure, does not require a
correction when using different units of measure.

Both Pratt (1964) and Arrow (1965, 1971) define a function that
is referred to now as the relative risk aversion measure. Pratt uses the
term the measure of proportional risk aversion for this function, but
Arrow's term, relative risk aversion, is that most frequently used today,
and that practice is followed here. The notation for this relative risk
aversion measure is $R(W)$, and $R(W)$ is defined by

$$R(W) = \frac{-u''(W)W}{u'(W)} = A(W) \cdot W$$

From $A(W)$ one can always obtain $R(W)$ by multiplying by W. The
reverse is also possible except at $W = 0$. Thus, except at $W = 0$, the
two functions are one to one and either multiplication or division can
be used to go from one measure to the other. Since $R(W)$ can easily
be converted to $A(W)$, $R(W)$ has the same advantages as does the
absolute risk aversion measure. $R(W)$ is a unique respresentation of
risk preferences, there are no arbitrary constants, and assuming monotonicity, one can divide $R(W)$ by W (except at $W = 0$), and use the
resulting $A(W)$ to determine the N-M utility function using the steps
that were just described (Eq. 2.1).

The relative risk aversion measure has the added advantage that its
value does not change when the outcome variable is measured using a
different unit of measure. $R(W)$ is an elasticity, it is the elasticity of
$u'(W)$, and it has the usual advantages of using elasticity rather than
slope when measuring the effect of change in a variable. The effect on
marginal utility of changing the value for the outcome variable is being
measured. In slope terms, this of course is given by $u''(W)$, which has
several disadvantages as a measure of risk preferences. The measure of
this same effect expressed in elasticity terms is given by $R(W)$. To see

this, rewrite $R(W)$ as

$$R(W) = \frac{-u''(W)W}{u'(W)} = \left(\frac{-u''(W)}{u'(W)}\right) \Big/ (1/W)$$

The numerator in the right side expression is the percentage change in marginal utility and the denominator is the percentage change in outcome variable W when W is changed one unit. The sign has been adjusted so that risk aversion gives a positive value for $R(W)$ when W is positive.

To confirm that changes in the unit of measure for W do not affect the relative risk aversion function, use the same example as above (Eq. 2.2) where $X = t \cdot W$. From this, it is easily confirmed that

$$R_v(X) = \frac{-v''(X)X}{v'(X)} = \frac{-u''(W)W}{u'(W)} = R_u(W)$$

Thus, utility functions $u(W)$ and $v(X)$, which represent the same risk preferences, but are different from one another because W and X are measured using different units, have exactly the same relative risk aversion measures. That is, the two relative risk aversion measures are equal when evaluated at comparable values, values for X and W where $W = t \cdot X$. Continuing the example used earlier, rate of return when expressed in percentage rather than decimal terms would change the absolute risk aversion measure by a factor of one hundred, but would not change the measure of relative risk aversion at all.

There is one particular aspect of relative risk aversion that one must be careful to recognize. With concave utility functions and positive measures of absolute risk aversion, the relative risk aversion measure, $R(W)$, takes on a negative value whenever the outcome variable does. Thus, requiring $R(W)$ to be a positive constant, for instance, makes no sense when the outcome variable W can take on both negative and positive values and risk aversion is assumed. Similarly, the requirement that $R(W)$ always decrease is problematic since with risk aversion, $R(W)$ changes sign from negative to positive as W passes through zero. Katz (1983), Briys and Eeckhoudt (1985) and Hey (1985) discuss and debate this point. More recently, Löffler (2001) illustrates a similiar point in a mean-variance context.

In the majority of the work examined here this peculiar property of the relative risk aversion measure is dealt with in one of two ways. In most cases, such as in the analysis of Arrow (1965, 1971) and Pratt (1964), the outcome variable itself is restricted to be nonnegative. For variables such as wealth or consumption this is a relatively natural and acceptable restriction and relative risk aversion continues as the main method of representing risk taking propensities. For other outcome variables, such as economic profit, where positive and negative values are possible and relevant, this pecularity is dealt with by focusing on the absolute rather than the relative risk aversion measure; that is, for outcome variables that can take on both positive and negative values, absolute risk aversion is usually employed when discussing and representing risk preferences.

Many other measures of risk aversion are possible. A few have already been defined and others may well be proposed in the future. When those measures are one to one with $A(W)$, as all defined so far are, these measures have all the advantages of $A(W)$, they are unique and complete representations of the risk preferences of the decision maker. Two such measures are briefly described below, and the rationale for these additional definitions is given. The discussion is very brief because for the purpose of presenting information concerning a decision maker's propensity to take risk, these additional measures do not prove very useful.

Soon after the work of Pratt (1964) and Arrow (1965, 1971), both Menezes and Hanson (1970), and Zeckhauser and Keeler (1970), introduce a definition which is now referred to as the definition of partial relative risk aversion. This measure has an additional parameter in its definition. The outcome variable is decomposed into two parts, W and X, where only W is random. With this, the measure of partial relative risk aversion $P(W; X)$, is defined by

$$P(W; X) = \frac{-u''(W + X)W}{u'(W + X)}$$

This measure falls in between the measures of absolute and relative risk aversion. There is a different partial risk aversion measure for each value for X.

Partial risk aversion, like relative risk aversion, is obtained from absolute risk aversion by multiplying by the outcome variable, but for partial risk aversion only the random portion of the outcome variable is used rather than all of it. It is easily verified that the absolute, relative and partial relative risk aversion measures are related by

$$P(W;X) = R(W + X) - X \cdot A(W + X)$$

Partial risk aversion can be derived from $A(W)$ and except at $W = 0$ the reverse is also the case, assuming that the value for X is known. Thus, the partial relative risk aversion function completely and uniquely represents the risk preferences of the decision maker as long as W is not zero and preferences for the outcome variable are monotonic, and the value for X is specified.

Why have these three different risk aversion functions been defined and used when, for the purposes of representing the risk preferences of the decision maker, the three measures are not very different? The answer to this question can be illustrated by examining the comparative static theorems in which conditions on these various measures of risk preferences are employed. For each of these three risk aversion measures there are theorems in the literature where a relatively simple condition on one of the measures of risk preferences is sufficient to demonstrate a finding that is consistent with observation. Such comparative static theorems are a significant part of the information that is available concerning the risk preferences of decision makers. Of course, the simple condition imposed on one risk aversion function can be stated instead in terms of either of the other two measures, but often not in nearly as simple or interpretable a fashion.

As an example of this, consider what may be the most well known theorem concerning portfolio choice. Assume a simple portfolio model where an investor begins with a certain level of wealth, W_0, and chooses to allocate a proportion of this wealth, α, to a risky investment whose return is random, and the remaining portion, $(1 - \alpha)$, to a riskless asset whose return is certain. In this model, it is well known that when relative risk aversion for wealth is a constant, then the optimal choice for α does not change with changes in the value for W_0. This condition on risk preferences, $R'(W) = 0$, is a very simple one to state and interpret.

If this same result were presented using absolute risk aversion to describe risk preferences, the condition imposed on absolute risk aversion would require that its derivative satisfy $A'(W) = -\theta/W^2$, where θ is the constant measure of relative risk aversion. This condition on risk preferences is equivalent to $R'(W) = 0$, but the latter condition concerning relative risk aversion is simpler and more easily interpreted than is the restriction on the slope of the absolute risk aversion measure. The case for simplicity is made even stronger in the more complete version of this theorem which indicates that α increases or decreases when W_0 is increased if $R(W)$ is decreasing or increasing, respectively. Stating this restriction in terms of the slope of absolute risk aversion requires that $A(W)$ be more or less steeply sloped than $(-\theta/W^2)$, hardly an intuitive restriction.

The example just given illustrates why relative risk aversion is a useful measure of risk preferences. Many similar examples exist which illustrate why absolute risk aversion and partial relative risk aversion are also useful. For absolute and relative risk aversion, examples are found in the work of Pratt (1964) and Arrow (1965, 1971), and in many other places. For partial relative risk aversion, these examples are found in the work that introduces the definition for that measure, and in other related papers. See particularly, Menezes and Hanson (1970), Zeckhauser and Keeler (1970), Diamond and Stiglitz (1974), Eeckhoudt and Gollier (1995), and Briys and Eeckhoudt (1985) for excellent examples concerning the usefulness of the partial relative risk aversion measure.

The last function mentioned here is risk tolerance, which is sometimes used to represent risk preferences for decision makers, and is used by Barsky et al. (1997) because of its aggregation properties. This makes risk tolerance particular well suited when discussing optimal risk sharing. An early paper in this area is that by Wilson (1968) and a current discussion and treatment of optimal risk sharing is presented by Eeckhoudt et al. (2005) in their Chapters 10 and 11. Risk tolerance is defined to be equal to $(1/R(W))$. One feature of this measure that one must be aware of involves the impact of averaging across samples. It is the case that the average of the risk tolerance measures across persons is not the same as one divided by the average of the relative risk aversion measures for those same persons. The average of the inverse is larger than the inverse of the average. This point is discussed further when the Barsky et al. (1997) findings are reviewed when discussing relative risk aversion for consumption in Section 4.

In summary, there are many functions that can be used to represent the risk preferences of expected utility maximizing decision makers. There is no one best function, and each of the alternatives has advantages and disadvantages. For each function there are uses for which the particular function is well suited. As stated at the very beginning, the purpose of this review is to consolidate on a common scale as much information concerning risk preferences as possible. For that purpose, the relative risk aversion measure is well suited, and superior to each of the other alternatives. Consequently relative risk aversion is the description of risk preferences used in the majority of this study.

2.2 Outcomes variables and their relationships

The key to understanding how information concerning risk aversion for different outcome variables is to be compared and consolidated is to have a good understanding of how the outcome variables themselves may be related. The purpose of this section is to establish the framework of analysis used for the consolidation of risk preference information for the various outcome variables that are encountered when reviewing information concerning risk aversion. This is accomplished by carefully working through several examples. These examples come from the literature that is reviewed in later sections. The three outcome variables that are considered are all of one dimension, and all can be related to the reference outcome variable, A-P wealth.

As pointed out earlier, the risk aversion information for each outcome variable is unique to that variable, and directly applies to only that variable. When one outcome variable can be linked to another, however, the risk aversion information for the one can be adjusted so that it applies to the other variable as well. In this survey, the functions linking outcome variables are sometimes established by analysis of the definitions or measures used for the outcome variables themselves, and in other instances are obtained by other means. The examples given illustrate both types of sources for this information.

The examples that are provided are a series of progressively more complicated relationships between a pair of outcome variables. One of the outcome variables in each of the pairs is the reference variable W, while the other outcome variable is different in each of the examples. The examples are chosen to be representative of the type of analysis and the relationships encountered when reviewing the literature. In each of these three examples, the two outcome variables are related in a deterministic manner. It is possible for the new outcome variable to be stochastically related to W and examples of this are discussed in Section 3.2.

One particular outcome variable plays a special role in the analysis, and is the starting point of the discussion. This outcome variable is referred to as Arrow-Pratt (A-P) wealth. A-P wealth is defined so that included with wealth is the value of all assets, and only those assets, whose quantities can be freely adjusted. This definition of wealth is consistent with that employed by Arrow (1965, 1971) and by Pratt (1964) in their discussion of absolute and relative risk aversion measures for utility from wealth. This definition of wealth is also the one most commonly used in the theoretical analysis of portfolio decisions.

The definition of A-P wealth is not an easy one to apply empirically. This is both because the degree to which the value associated with an asset can be reallocated varies continously and is not often zero or one, and also because data is frequently not available on the value for all assets. Most empirical measures of wealth fail to include some assets whose value may be part of A-P wealth, and likely also do include the values of other assets when that value may be difficult and costly to reallocate to other assets. Thus, A-P wealth should be viewed as an ideal, and unlikely to ever be measured perfectly in empirical studies.

The notation used for the outcome variable called A-P wealth is W. It is assumed that the possible values for A-P wealth range from zero to some upper limit denoted $\overline{W}$, and that the N-M utility function $u(W)$ exists for this outcome variable. With the monotonicity condition, $u(W)$ then takes values in the interval $\left[u(0), u(\overline{W})\right]$. The choice of zero as the lowest possible value for W is made primarily for convenience, but it is also the case that both Arrow (1965, 1971) and Pratt (1964) do assume that wealth is nonnegative.

There are many other outcome variables in addition to A-P wealth that are encountered in the literature concerning the risk taking propensity of decision makers. For many of these outcome variables one can determine a function relating one outcome variable to another one. If so, this function can be used to determine the relationship between the relative risk aversion measures for the two outcome variables. Sometimes the function relating outcome variables is quite obvious and comes from their definitions, and in other instances the relationship is less clear. The following three examples illustrate each situation.

Example 2.1 One of the simplest relationships between two outcome variables that can occur can be illustrated in a basic portfolio model. In this model it is assumed that all of initial wealth can be freely allocated among assets, and that the value of those assets in the future is random. Assume further that the allocation is selected by the decision maker so as to maximize expected utility from final wealth. In this model, the outcome variable is A-P wealth and is denoted W.

One can represent this exact same decision using a different outcome variable. Again it is assumed that wealth can be freely allocated among the various assets, but to determine which allocation is best, the decison maker is assumed to maximize expected utility from return on investment, denoted Y. Now return, Y, is defined by the equation

$$Y = \frac{W}{W_0}$$

This equation defining Y provides the equation that relates the two outcome variables, Y and W, to one another. In this example, outcome variables Y and W are scalar multiples of one another. Given this function relating Y and W, the utility function for Y and for W, $v(Y)$

and $u(W)$, must satisfy the equation[3]

$$v(Y) = v\left(\frac{W}{W_0}\right) = u(W)$$

Earlier, when discussing the advantages of using the relative risk aversion function to represent and measure risk preferences, it was noted that the relative risk aversion measures for these two utility functions, $v(Y)$ and $u(W)$, are the same when evaluated at $Y = \frac{W}{W_0}$. That is, since these two outcome variables are scalar multiples of one another, their risk aversion measures are the same when evaluated at the appropriate points for each. Thus, for this example

$$R_v(Y) = \frac{-v''(Y)Y}{v'(Y)} = \frac{-u''(W)W}{u'(W)} = R_u(W)$$

whenever $Y = \frac{W}{W_0}$.

Example 2.2   A second example with a somewhat more complicated relationship between outcome variables is illustrated by examining the outcome variable that is natural to use when the gains and losses from investing are taxed at fixed rate t. In this case, after tax wealth may well be the natural outcome variable of concern to the decision maker. This outcome variable, after-tax wealth, is denoted W_t and is defined by the following equation. The portfolio setting is one with a single risky and riskless asset.

$$W_t = W_0(1 - t)(\alpha(r - 1) + (1 - \alpha)(\rho - 1)) + W_0$$

In this equation, W_0 represents the initial wealth of the investor, t is the tax rate on investment gains or losses, α is the proportion of initial wealth invested in the risky asset whose return is r and rate of return is $(r - 1)$, and $(\rho - 1)$ is the rate of return on the riskless asset. Notice

---

[3] Assuming the two utility functions must satisfy this relationship assumes that two outcomes, such as $Y = 1.1$ or $W = (1.1)W_0$, which lead to the same consequence, must give the same utility. Rubinstein (2006) argues that such an assumption is not required as part of the axioms of expected utility.

that the expression indicates that it is the investment gain or loss, not wealth itself that is taxed.

To determine the relationship between W_t and W, consider this same portfolio decision without taxes, the case where $t = 0$. This equation is given below and defines W.

$$W = W_0(\alpha(r - 1) + (1 - \alpha)(\rho - 1)) + W_0$$

Making use of these two expressions one can determine the function that expresses the relationship between the outcome variables where one ignores taxes and the other includes them. This function relating W and W_t is given below.

$$W_t = t \cdot W_0 + (1 - t)W$$

This function indicates that after-tax wealth and A-P wealth are linearly related, but are not proportional to one another. This is because investment gains and losses, and not wealth, is taxed.

The function relating W and W_t allows one to determine the pairs of before tax wealth outcomes and after tax wealth outcomes that correspond to one another. For instance, if initial wealth W_0 is 100 and the tax rate t is 0.5, then a lottery with before tax outcomes of $W = 110$ or $W = 120$ corresponds to a lottery with $W_t = 105$ or $W_t = 110$ as outcomes when after tax wealth is the outcome variable. It is assumed that the decision maker is indifferent between receiving these corresponding quantities. That is, it is assumed that a lottery yielding $W = 110$ or 120 with equal probability and a lottery yielding $W_t = 105$ or 110 with equal probability give the same expected utility and are ranked the same by the decision maker. This assumption allows the function relating W to W_t to be used to determine the relationships between the utility functions for these two outcome variables, and hence their relative risk aversion measures as well.

Specifically, given that outcome variables W and W_t are related by $W_t = t \cdot W_0 + (1 - t)W$, it is then the case that their utility functions satisfy

$$v(W_t) = v(t \cdot W_0 + (1 - t)W) = u(W)$$

Taking the first and second derivatives of both sides of this equation gives

$$u'(W) = v'(W_t)(1 - t)$$

and

$$u''(W) = v''(W_t)(1 - t)^2$$

These first and second derivative relationships and the relationship between the outcome variables can be used to obtain the function relating the relative risk aversion measures for outcome variables W and W_t. Two different ways to express this function are given below.

$$R_u(W) = R_v(W_t) \cdot \frac{W}{W_t}(1 - t)$$

or

$$R_u(W) = R_v(W_t)\frac{(W_t - t \cdot W_0)}{W_t}$$

In these equations, $R_u(W)$ denotes the relative risk aversion measure for outcome variable W and $R_v(W_t)$ is that same risk aversion measure for outcome variable W_t.

As the reader can observe, even this simple linear relationship between outcome variables W and W_t translates into a relatively complex expression relating their relative risk aversion measures. In this example, the magnitudes of the two relative risk aversion measures differ even when evaluated at their corresponding values. In addition, it is the case that the slopes of the two relative risk aversion measure are not the same, and may not even have the same sign. When $R_u(W)$ is a constant, for instance, $R_v(W_t)$ must be negatively sloped, and when $R_v(W_t)$ is a constant, $R_u(W)$ must be positively sloped. Near the end of this section a general result, Theorem 2.4, gives even more details concerning the relationship between the relative risk aversion measures for linearly related outcome variables.

An additional point can be illustrated with this same example and pair of outcome variables. This point is that changing an outcome variable also changes well known theorems in ways that are not always recognized or obvious. Recall the portfolio theorem mentioned earlier. This theorem indicates that constant relative risk aversion for outcome variable W, implies that a change in initial wealth has no effect on the decision maker's choice of allocation between the risky and riskless assets.

This theorem is correct, but it is important to recognize that it applies to outcome variable W which ignores the taxation of investment income. When investment gains or losses are taxed, and the decision maker maximizes expected utility from W_t rather than W, then it is $R_v(W_t)$ not $R_u(W)$ which must be constant in order that changes in W_0 leave α unaffected. As the relationships between the relative risk aversion measures for these two outcome variables indicates, $R_v(W_t)$ can only be a constant if $R_u(W)$ is an increasing function. Thus, if one observes that changes in initial wealth do not alter the proportions allocated to risky and riskless assets in a setting where investment gains and losses are taxed, increasing relative risk aversion for A-P wealth is required to explain this observation. When using evidence concerning risk aversion derived from theoretical analysis, one must be sensitive to the outcome variable used in the analysis. Changing the outcome variable in theoretical derivations can alter the conditions on risk aversion measures assumed in those derivations.

Example 2.3   The two examples that were just presented determine the function defining the relationship between a pair of outcome variables in a rather mechanical way using the definitions of those variables. The function that is obtained specifies the relationship between the two outcome variables, and this relationship holds true for all decision makers, and does not vary across decision makers. In the final example, the function relating the two outcomes variables is not so easily obtained, and not all will agree that the function chosen is the correct one. In addition, in the specific settings given here where this function is clearly the correct one to use, the relationship depends on the risk preferences of the decision maker and is specific to that decision maker. The example is presented to illustrate the methodology employed when attempting to consolidate risk preference information for outcome variables when the function relating the outcome variables is less than obvious.

The last example that is discussed includes two outcome variables, A-P wealth, and one that is referred to as consumption and denoted C. Consumption, as defined or measured in the research that is reviewed, is usually a quite broad measure, and is measured in monetary units just as is wealth. Consumption consists of the value of all of the goods the consumer chooses to use up or consume during a particular time period or at a point in time. Thus, consumption has many of the same measurement difficulties as does A-P wealth. The components to include with consumption can be a decision that must be made, and data availability may limit which values for consumed goods are included when measuring consumption.

Research concerning optimal consumption and how optimal consumption depends on other variables often provides information concerning the magnitude of the relative risk aversion measure for the outcome variable consumption. The definitions of the two outcome variables C and W do not appear to provide much of a hint as to the form or exact nature of a function relating these two outcome variables. Therefore, other sources for this function must be used. The choice made here is to examine economic models where both C and W are variables, and to determine a relationship between these two variables within those models. The focus is on models of the consumer where the consumer chooses an optimal level of consumption, and this optimal value for C depends in part on the wealth of the consumer.

In the models that are considered, the decision maker is assumed to maximize utility from consumption over a number of time periods. The goods that make up consumption in each time period are acquired and paid for using many sources of funds. These sources of funds include such things as labor income and transfer payments, but also include the return earned on invested wealth. The decision maker's choice of an optimal consumption level in each time period then depends on the levels of all of these sources of funds, and specifically depends on the wealth of the consumer. Overall, consumption choices are limited by a lifetime budget constraint. The wealth variable used in these models of multi-period consumption is assumed to be freely allocable if portfolio decisions are also made, and hence is interpreted as A-P wealth and denoted W.

When the consumer maximizes the expected utility from consumption, solving the optimization problem determines the optimal level of consumption in each time period. This optimal level of C depends on the values of the various other variables in the model, including the level of W. It is this function, relating C to W, that is used here to specify a function relating C and W so that the utility functions and relative risk aversion measures for these two outcome variables can be related as well.

Not many models of multi-period consumption determine an explicit function relating optimal consumption to the other variables in the analysis. Two models where this function relating C to W is explicitly derived are used here to suggest the general properties of that function. Two models of multi-period consumption with a sufficiently simple formulation and strong enough assumptions to allow derivation of the function relating C and W are those presented by Kimball and Mankiw (1989) (K-M) and by Meyer and Meyer (2005a) (M-M). K-M and M-M each begin with a different specific form for utility from consumption, and each make different assumptions concerning which parameters in the model are random and which are not, and yet derive functions relating C to W that are quite similar to one another. The general form of this relationship is used here as the starting point in determining a function relating consumption to wealth.

Although they differ in many details, K-M and M-M each model a consumer who maximizes the expected value of the discounted sum of utility from consumption from a number of time periods. Both models include wealth in the analysis. Consumers receive income in each period, and can consume from this income and from wealth saved from previous periods. Their consumption choices are limited by a lifetime budget constraint. Wealth in these models is accumulated so as to smooth lifetime consumption. In this context, K-M and M-M each determine that the optimal value for consumption in each period is linearly related to the wealth at the beginning of the time period. Both find that the additive and multiplicative coefficients in the linear specification are each positive. That is, the marginal propensity to consume from wealth is positive, and the positive additive constant represents the use of wealth to smooth consumption across time periods.

Thus, the assumption is made here that outcome variables C and W are related by a linear function $C = a + b \cdot W$, where both a and b are positive numbers. This assumption is discussed further when information concerning the relative risk aversion measure for consumption is reviewed in detail in Section 4. In that analysis, additional research is examined to determine appropriate values for the coefficients in this linear function. For now the linear nature of the function is all that is needed.

Notice that in this third example, the relationship between outcomes variables is not more complicated than the previous example, it is also a linear relationship, but now the source for the function relating the two outcome variables is quite different. Rather than relating outcome variables on the basis of their definitions, a procedure that gives the same answer for each decision maker, the function relating C to W is determined for a specific set of risk preferences. Thus, even though $C = a + b \cdot W$ is used to describe the relationship between C and W, the use of this function is certainly subject to debate, the magnitudes of the coefficients in the linear function are not easily determined, and exactly which linear function to use could be revised by further research.

To complete the discussion, when $C = a + b \cdot W$, utility for consumption and utility for wealth must be related by

$$v(C) = v(a + b \cdot W) = u(W)$$

With this relationship between utility functions, the relative risk aversion for A-P wealth and that for consumption are related by the equation

$$R_u(W) = \frac{b \cdot W}{(a + b \cdot W)} R_v(C)$$

Using estimated values for the two parameters, a and b, this function relating relative risk aversion for consumption and relative risk aversion for wealth can be used to convert information concerning the relative risk aversion measure for either outcome variable to that of the other. This conversion is discussed further in Section 4 which deals with relative risk aversion for consumption.

The discussion in this section concludes with some general notation concerning outcome variables and functions indicating how they are related. Since a linear relationship between outcome variables is a simple and relevant one, a theorem from the literature connecting the relative risk aversion measure for linearly related outcome variables is also stated. Most of the analysis here focuses on this linear case.

Outcome variables are denoted by capital letters. When representing the relationship between those outcome variables, the same capital letters are used to denote the functions relating the variables. For instance, the relationship between after-tax wealth and A-P wealth is written as $W_t = W_t(W) = t \cdot W_0 + (1 - t)W$, and the relationship between consumption and wealth is given as $C = C(W) = a + b \cdot W$. In general, for any pair of outcome variables X and Y, the relationship between them is given as $Y = Y(X)$.

Given the relationship between outcome variables, $Y = Y(X)$, the utility functions for these two outcome variables are related by $v(Y) = v(Y(X)) = u(X)$. This implies that

$$u'(X) = v'(Y) \cdot Y'(X)$$

and

$$u''(X) = v''(X) \cdot (Y'(X))^2 + v'(Y) \cdot Y''(X)$$

The steps below convert this information about relationships between first and second derivatives of $u(X)$ and $v(Y)$ into the expression relating their relative risk aversion measures. The arguments of the $Y(X)$, $Y'(X)$ and $Y''(X)$ functions are suppressed to simplify notation.

$$R_u(X) = \frac{-u''(X) \cdot X}{u'(X)} = \frac{[-v''(Y)(Y'^2 - v'(Y) \cdot Y'']X}{v'(Y) \cdot Y'}$$

$$R_u(X) = \frac{-v''(Y)Y \cdot X \cdot Y'}{v'(Y) \cdot Y} - \frac{Y'' \cdot X}{Y'}$$

$$R_u(X) = R_v(Y)\frac{(X \cdot Y')}{Y} - \frac{Y'' \cdot X}{Y'}$$

The last equation gives the relationship between the relative risk aversion measures for outcome variables X and Y. The last term on the right hand side of this equation is the equivalent of the relative risk aversion measure for the function $Y(X)$. It is the elasticity of the slope of this function. Notice though that even when $Y(X)$ is linear so that $Y''(X) = 0$ and this last term disappears, the relative risk aversion measures for $u(X)$ and $v(Y)$ still differ in both magnitude and slope. The two relative risk aversion measures are only the same when Y is proportional to X.

In each of the examples given above, a linear function describing the relationship between outcome variables is determined. It is also the case that when evaluating empirically derived relative risk aversion measures, the measurement differences that are encountered involve including or excluding components of variables in one study but not another. This also leads to a relationship between Y and X that is a linear one. For these reasons, the linear case warrants special attention and notation.

Assume that $Y = a + b \cdot X$. Using the general relationship for $Y = Y(X)$ that was just presented, this implies that the relationship between the relative risk aversion measures for these two outcome variables is given by

$$R_u(X) = R_v(Y) \left[\frac{bX}{a + bX} \right] = R_v(Y) \left[\frac{bX}{Y} \right]$$

A theorem which makes several comparisons implied by this relationship between these two risk aversion measures is given in Meyer and Meyer (2005a) and reproduced without proof below.

Theorem 2.4 If $Y = a + b \cdot X$ with $a > 0$ and $b > 0$, then
   a) $R_u(X) \leq R_v(Y)$
   b) $R_u'(X) > 0$ when $R_v'(Y) = 0$ and $R_v'(Y) < 0$ when $R_u'(X) = 0$
   c) $\dfrac{R_u'(X) \cdot X}{R_u(X)} = \left[\dfrac{bX}{Y} \right] \left[\dfrac{R_v'(Y) \cdot Y}{R_v(Y)} \right] + \left[\dfrac{a}{Y} \right]$ [1]

   d) $\dfrac{R_u'(X) \cdot X}{R_u(X)} \geq \dfrac{R_v'(Y) \cdot Y}{R_v(Y)}$ if and only if $v(Y)$ displays decreasing absolute risk aversion

---

The restriction $Y = a + b \cdot X$ with $a > 0$ and $b > 0$ is separated into two cases for discussion purposes. When $Y = a + b \cdot X$ and $a > 0$ and $b > 1$, the outcome variable Y includes terms not in X represented by the additive constant, and also may include additional terms that are proportional to X. For this case, Y is referred to as more inclusively defined or measured than is X. For the second case where $a > 0$ and $0 < b < 1$, outcome Y is less variable than X. In interpreting the findings presented in Theorem 2.4, the discussion will frequently use the phrase "more inclusively measured or less risky" to denote the general restriction in the theorem that $Y = a + b \cdot X$ with $a > 0$ and $b > 0$.

Property (a) of Theorem 2.4 indicates that the relative risk aversion measure associated with an outcome variable is larger when the outcome variable is measured more inclusively or is less risky. This property is the only one that deals with the magnitude of relative risk aversion. The remaining three properties each deal with either the slope or the elasticity of the relative risk aversion measures.

Property (b) indicates that constant relative risk aversion is not possible for both outcome variables even for this case of linearly related outcome variables unless the variables are proportional to one another. In addition, property (b) indicates that when the relative risk aversion measure for the more inclusive or less risky outcome variable is constant, then that for the less inclusive and riskier variable must be increasing. The opposite is also true. When relative risk aversion for the less inclusive and riskier variable is constant, then that for the other outcome variable must be decreasing. The after-tax wealth and consumption examples illustrate this. Relative risk aversion for after tax wealth W_t or consumption C can only be constant if relative risk aversion for A-P wealth is increasing. Alternatively, when the relative risk aversion measure for W is constant, then the relative risk aversion measure for either W_t or C must be decreasing.

Properties (c) and (d) discuss the relationship between the elasticities rather than slopes of the relative risk aversion measures. Property (c) states that the more inclusive or less risky an outcome variable is, the further its elasticity is from one. Stated differently, the less inclusive and riskier outcome variable has an elasticity that is a convex combination of the elasticity of the more inclusive and less risky variable and the number one.

Property (d) expands on property (c) using the fact that if absolute risk aversion is decreasing, then the elasticity of relative risk aversion is less than one. Thus, with this additional condition on absolute risk aversion, it is the case that elasticity of the relative risk aversion measure for the more inclusive or less risky variable is always smaller than that for the less inclusive or more risky variable. Theorem 2.4 is referred to often in the discussion in the remainder of the paper. In this discussion properties (b), (c) and (d) are loosely summarized by stating that the slope and elasticity of the relative risk aversion measure for the more inclusive and less risky outcome variables tend to be smaller than those for the less inclusive and riskier outcome variables.

2.3   The choice set assumptions

To carry out the analysis that relates the relative risk aversion measures for pairs of outcome variables, an important assumption concerning the choice set over which lotteries are defined and to which the axioms of expected utility apply is being made. This section states and discusses that assumption. It does so because the assumption is not one which all would be willing to make, and most would not be willing to make this particular assumption in all decision settings. There certainly is evidence that the assumption is violated in some situations. In spite of this, the assumption is made here as it is crucial when consolidating risk preference information for a variety of outcome variables.

In the analysis in Section 2.2, a function relating outcome variables is used to define the relationship between the utility functions and relative risk aversion measures for those outcome variables. This step in the analysis assumes that the various possible values for each of the outcome variables are elements of a single choice set or prize space to which the axioms of expected utility apply. To help understand what this means, the assumption is first illustrated and discussed using just two outcome variables, W and W_t, and then the assumption is stated for the general case of many outcome variables.

Recall the discussion in Example 2.2 of the previous section where the relationship between $R_u(W)$ and $R_v(W_t)$, the relative risk aversion measures for two different measures of wealth, W and W_t, is derived. There are two steps in that analysis. The first step examines the definitions of W and W_t, and uses these definitions to determine an equation that relates the two outcome variables to one another. This step does not involve expected utility. The second step takes this function relating outcome variables, and uses it first to determine an equation relating the utility functions for these outcome variables, $v(W_t)$ and $u(W)$, and then from this equation calculates the relationship between $R_u(W)$ and $R_v(W_t)$. To carry out this second step, the utility functions for these two outcome variables must exist, and must be related to one another in the manner indicated. The existence of these utility functions, and the relationship between them is implied by an assumption concerning the choice set faced by the decision maker.

To ensure that the utility functions $u(W)$ and $v(W_t)$ exist and represent the risk preferences of one decision maker, the axioms of expected utility can be assumed to apply to a choice set containing outcomes that are quantities of W and quantities of W_t. That is, the decision maker is assumed to choose among lotteries or probability distributions defined over a choice set denoted S, where S contains ordered pairs (W, W_t). It is important to recognize that S includes all ordered pairs where either W or W_t is equal to zero. Whether set S contains all ordered pairs (W, W_t) or only those where either W or W_t equals zero does not matter, the later is sufficient. When the axioms of expected utility apply to this set S, there exists a function, $U(W, W_t)$, defined on S, which is the decision maker's N-M utility for ranking probability distributions over outcomes in set S.

Now $U(W, W_t)$ is a function of two outcome variables rather than one. It can be used, however, to define two utility functions of only one variable each. This is accomplished by considering only outcomes and lotteries over those outcomes where either W or W_t is zero. For these lotteries, the expected utility ranking of the lotteries can be represented by two utility functions each defined over just one outcome variable. The utility function defined over two dimensions, $U(W, W_t)$, is reduced to two separate and different utility functions of one dimension. Specifically, these two utility functions over one dimension are denoted $u(W)$ and $v(W_t)$, and are defined by $u(W) = U(W, 0)$ and $v(W_t) = U(0, W_t)$. Assuming that the axioms of expected utility apply to choice set S ensures the existence of the two utility function $u(W)$ and $v(W_t)$, and also implies that the risk preferences being represented and investigated are those for one decision maker. This is the assumption that allows information concerning the relative risk aversion measure for one outcome variable to also provide information concerning the relative risk aversion measure for another.

To generalize this assumption to more that two outcome variables is a relatively easy task. The choice set S to which the axioms of expected utility apply is assumed to be a subset of R_n, where n denotes the number of different outcome variables that are considered. Choice set S includes elements where the quantities of at least $(n-1)$ of the outcome variables are zero. The same procedure as in the two variable example is then used to define n different functions of one variable that represent the risk taking propensities of the decision maker when the lotteries being ranked involved one and only one of the outcome variables. These functions exist and represent the risk preferences of one individual whenever the axioms of expected utility apply to the choice set S.

In the first example presented in Section 2.2, where the outcome variables are wealth and return, the discussion presented there emphasizes the fact that the analysis assumes that when wealth equals W, or return Y equals $\frac{W}{W_0}$, the decision maker considered these two outcomes to be equivalent. Another way to say this is that the decision maker assigns these two outcomes the same level of utility. That is when rate of return $Y = \frac{W}{W_0}$, then $U(W,0) = U\left(0, \frac{W}{W_0}\right)$ or equivalently $u(W) = v\left(\frac{W}{W_0}\right) = v(Y)$.

Similarly, when discussing the second example involving outcome variables W and W_t, it was emphasized that two different outcomes, where one is in terms of wealth, and the other is in terms of after-tax wealth, give the same utility as long as those outcomes are related to one another by the equation $W_t = t \cdot W_0 + (1-t)W$. In the notation here, it was assumed that $U(W,0)$ equals $U(0,W_t)$ for values for W and W_t satisfying this function. Again this implies that $u(W) = v(W_t)$.

When relating A-P wealth to either after-tax wealth or return, the assumption that these outcome variables are part of a single choice choice set is not likely to be controversial or questioned. Some may even consider such preferences to be the basis for rational behavior.

For those two pairs of outcome variables, the function relating the outcome variable to W comes from their definition. For the third pair of outcome variables, W and C, and many others, however, the validity of this assumption concerning the choice set of the decision maker may be questioned, and the implied relationship between relative risk aversion measures may not be universally accepted.

The assumption concerning choice set S also allows the analysis to be reversed. That is, the relationship between utility functions and relative risk aversion measures for any two outcome variables can be used to define a function relating those outcome variables when the assumption concerning choice set S holds. Suppose for instance that the relationship $R_u(W) = R_v(W_t)\frac{(W_t - t \cdot W_0)}{W_t}$ is determined to hold between the relative risk aversion measures for W and W_t. If these two outcome variable are part of one choice set S, this can only be the case if their two utility functions are related by $v(W_t) = v(t \cdot W_0 + (1 - t)W) = u(W)$, and this in turn implies that $W_t = t \cdot W_0 + (1 - t)W$. When utility functions $u(W)$ and $v(W_t)$ are known, and these two utility functions represent the risk taking propensities of one decision maker ranking elements of a single choice set containing elements of the form $(W, 0)$ and $(0, W_t)$, then $W_t = v^{-1}(u(W))$ defines the relationship between the two outcome variables. That is, when utility functions are known to be for a single set of risk preferences, the relationship between the utility functions can be used to derive the underlying relationship between the outcome variables themselves.

Research has shown that decision makers sometimes do not satisfy this assumption of having preferences over a single choice set S containing as elements quantities of different outcome variables. Evidence indicates that there are outcome variables and decision makers such that the values for one outcome variable and those for another are not elements of the same choice set to which the axioms of expected utility apply. Terms such as framing or consequentialism are sometimes used to describe when this is the case. Similarly, it is sometimes claimed that a decision maker can fail to integrate some components of wealth, such as that associated with human capital or transfer payments, when making portfolio decisions. In such cases, even though there may be a function relating outcome variables X and Y, the decision maker does not treat as equivalent, payoffs that are implied to be equivalent by this function; that is, the assumption concerning choice set S is not satisfied.

An example of such an instance is the following. Suppose a person is given USD10 as an initial payment, and then asked to choose between two lotteries L_1 and L_2. L_1 pays USD -5 or USD $+15$ with equal probability and L_2 pays USD8 for sure. Suppose the person chooses L_2. Now assume that instead of giving the person an initial payment of USD10, the lotteries are changed so that L_3 has outcomes of USD5 or USD25 with equal probability and L_4 offers USD18 for sure. The relationship between the outcome variables in this case, indicates that since L_2 is selected over L_1, then L_4 must be chosen over L_3. If the outcome variable in L_3 and L_4 is denoted Y and that in L_1 and L_2 is denoted X, then $Y = X + 10$. Thus, when the person is given USD10 to start before choosing between L_1 and L_2, the first pair of lotteries are equivalent to the second pair. It is the case that not all decision makers treat these pairs of lotteries as equivalent. The point of this example is that it may well be that not all decision makers integrate all outcome variables into a single choice set S over which the axioms of expected utility apply. Nonetheless, to adjust and integrate information concerning relative risk aversion for various outcome variables, it is useful to assume that they do so, and that assumption is made in the analysis presented here.

2.4   Miscellaneous

Evidence concerning the relative risk aversion function for individual agents comes mainly from experimental data where multiple decisions can be observed, and from theoretical analysis and comparative static theorems. The comparative static evidence indicates which restrictions on the slope and/or magnitude of risk aversion leads to predictions that match observation. Rarely is a formal empirical test of whether or not the prediction matches observation conducted. This methodology is used extensively to provide information concerning the slope and magnitude of risk aversion for the various risk aversion measures for individual decision makers.

Empirical evidence concerning the relative risk aversion function of individual decision makers is quite rare. Most often the data only provides information concerning the individual decision maker's choice one time from a particular choice set. From this single observation only one parameter of the relative risk aversion function can be determined, and usually the level of risk aversion is the parameter selected. Thus, there is evidence concerning the magnitude of relative risk aversion for individual decision makers.

These same empirical studies go on to determine how this magnitude of relative risk aversion for the individual varies with individual characteristics. How risk aversion varies with age, sex, marital status and other such parameters has been studied. In some instances, one of the characteristics of the individual is the level of the outcome variable itself. When this is the case, how relative risk aversion changes with this characteristic is used to provide evidence concerning the slope of relative risk aversion. Of course, this information is for the slope of relative risk aversion for a representative agent, not any particular individual decision maker. The majority of the empirical evidence that is available concerning the slope of risk aversion measures is of this form.

For example, the level of an individual's relative risk aversion measure can be determined from the individual's allocation to risky and riskless assets. How this level varies within the sample population with the individual's level of wealth is then interpreted as providing information concerning the slope of the relative risk aversion measure, but this slope is for a representative agent. Such an interpretation requires that how the level of relative risk aversion varies with a parameter such as wealth, is indicative of how the relative risk aversion measure for the individual varies with wealth of the individual. Estimating the relative risk aversion function for a representative decision maker in this way is common practice.

In theoretical analysis and in empirical work, the focus is on the magnitude and the slope of absolute and relative risk aversion. From the slope information it is also usually possible to also provide information concerning the elasticity of relative risk aversion. Thus, the discussion here focuses on just these three parameters of a relative risk aversion function. The value for these three parameters vary depending on where along the relative risk aversion function the parameter value is taken. It is usual to report these values at either the mean or median value of the outcome variable. Other aspects of risk aversion measures are sometimes restricted in the theoretical literature. Kimball (1993), for instance, defines standard risk aversion and Gollier and Pratt (1996) define risk vulnerability by placing additional restrictions on the risk preferences of the decision maker.

3

Relative Risk Aversion for Wealth

3.1 Arrow-Pratt wealth

Of all of the various outcome variables and risk aversion measures that exist in the literature, the relative risk aversion measure for A-P wealth is probably the most well known and most often discussed. In part, this is because Arrow (1965, 1971) and Pratt (1964) introduce their definitions of absolute and relative risk aversion for this particular outcome variable, and in part this is because for many decision makers, such as those making portfolio choices or insurance purchase decisions, it is natural to assume that the optimal decision is made to maximize expected utility from wealth.

Wealth in these decision models is a stock variable. In the majority of the analysis discussed here, the distinction between stocks and flows is unimportant because the decision being represented is assumed to occur just one time rather than being one choice in a sequence of decisions. It is the case, however, that some information concerning relative risk aversion for wealth comes from analysis within a multi-period consumption model where wealth is a stock, and both income flows and consumption flows are other important variables in the model.

As was indicated in the introduction, the reference variable selected in this review is referred to as Arrow-Pratt (A-P) wealth, and is defined so that included with A-P wealth is the value of all assets, and only those assets, whose quantities can be freely adjusted. This outcome variable was discussed extensively by Arrow (1965, 1971) and by Pratt (1964) and that discussion is summarized first. The notation for A-P wealth is W, and any variation in the definition or measure of wealth from this definition of A-P wealth is represented by placing a subscript on W.

For outcome variable A-P wealth, Arrow (1965, 1971) suggests two hypotheses concerning the slopes of the absolute and relative risk aversion measures. The first is that the measure of absolute risk aversion is decreasing in W, and the second is that the measure of relative risk aversion is increasing. Arrow argues that this is likely to be the case for most if not all decision makers, and argues more strongly for the first hypothesis than the second. Pratt's work also supports the hypothesis that absolute risk aversion for W is decreasing, but is more neutral concerning the slope of relative risk aversion. These two hypotheses concerning measures of risk aversion are quoted often, but sometimes are used inappropriately by applying them to outcome variables which are different from W.

A portion of the evidence that Arrow (1965, 1971) and Pratt (1964) provide to support these hypotheses involves determining how the slope of a risk aversion measure alters the comparative static effect of an increase in wealth on the value for a choice variable selected by a decision maker. For example, they show that a decision maker would choose to hold more of a risky asset as initial wealth increases if absolute risk aversion is decreasing, but would hold less of the risky asset when absolute risk aversion is increasing.

Arrow (1965, 1971) and Pratt (1964) use several different decision models including the portfolio model to show that assumptions concerning the slope of absolute or relative risk aversion affect the reaction of the decision maker to increases or decreases in initial wealth. They then argue that certain reactions that depend on the slope of risk aversion are consistent with what is observed, while others are not. This information is considered to be support for certain assumptions concerning the slopes of risk aversion measures, and also a basis for the rejection of other assumptions. This particular method of supporting a property of a risk aversion measure has been used frequently in the expected utility literature, and forms a basis for much of what is known concerning the absolute and relative risk aversion measures for A-P wealth.

Arrow (1965, 1971) and Pratt (1964) develop expressions showing how the risk premium, insurance premium and probability premium are related to the decision maker's measures of absolute and relative risk aversion. These premia are precisely defined reactions by the decision maker to the risk that he or she faces. In each case, how the premium depends on W is determined, and shown to be inversely related to W when the decision maker exhibits decreasing absolute risk aversion. For instance, the amount a decision maker is willing to pay for insurance which eliminates risk, called the insurance premium, depends on W, and this amount falls as W increases whenever the decision maker exhibits decreasing absolute risk aversion. The reverse is also true. When the decision maker is increasing absolute risk averse, an increase in W implies an increased willingness to pay for insurance for a fixed risk.

The details of arguments such as this one concerning insurance premiums can be found in the work of Arrow (1965, 1971) and Pratt (1964). Their analysis is deemed to provide significant support for the property of risk preferences called decreasing absolute risk aversion for W, and the large number of theorems published since the work of Arrow and Pratt have only added to the support for this property. Decreasing absolute risk aversion for outcome variable W is the usual assumption made in economic analysis, and increasing absolute risk aversion for W is quite universally rejected.

In addition to the risk, insurance and probability premia, Arrow (1965, 1971) and Pratt (1964) also use a simple portfolio model to determine how a decision maker's reaction to risk depends on the level of initial wealth. This portfolio model has been extensively analyzed by many others to provide additional information concerning risk aversion for wealth so it is presented in more detail. There are several formulations of the model that are in use. The one given below uses the same notation as that employed when discussing the relationship between before and after-tax wealth in Section 2.2. The model itself is written more compactly, however, because there is no longer a need to identify the rates of return separately from returns so that the taxation of the gains and losses from investment can be correctly represented. This portfolio model assumes that final wealth W is given by:

$$W = W_0(\alpha \cdot r + (1 - \alpha)\rho)$$

Recall that W_0 represents initial wealth, α is the proportion of wealth invested in the risky asset and r and ρ are the return to the risky and riskless assets, respectively.

For this portfolio decision, Arrow (1965, 1971) and Pratt (1964) show that (αW_0), the amount invested in the risky asset, increases (decreases) as W_0 increases, whenever the decision maker is decreasing (increasing) absolute risk averse. This finding adds to those concerning the risk, insurance and probability premia, and further supports the assumption of decreasing absolute risk aversion for outcome variable W.

The portfolio model is the usual setting where evidence concerning the slope of relative risk aversion for W is also discussed. The main theorem providing information concerning the slope of relative risk aversion in this portfolio model relates α, the proportion of wealth invested in the risky asset, to W_0. This theorem indicates that α decreases (increases) as W_0 is increased, whenever the decision maker exhibits increasing (decreasing) relative risk aversion. Of course, when relative risk aversion is a constant, α does not changes when W_0 changes. This is perhaps the most well known result concerning the slope of relative risk aversion for W in the literature. Arrow (1965, 1971) cites evidence concerning the elasticity of the demand for cash, interpreted as demand for the riskless asset, to support the hypothesis of increasing relative risk aversion.

Additional information concerning relative risk aversion is also obtained when one restates the finding concerning decreasing absolute risk aversion in relative risk aversion terms. This restatement indicates that if the relative risk aversion measure does not increase too rapidly, not faster than W, then the allocation to the risky asset increases as W_0 increases. Notice that this finding is for the absolute allocation to the risky asset, not the proportion allocated to that asset.

A symmetric finding where the absolute amount allocated to the riskless rather than the risky asset is required to increase with increases in W_0 can also be demonstrated. The condition required is that relative risk aversion not decrease too rapidly. As long the rate at which the relative risk aversion measure decreases is not too rapid, then the allocation to the riskless asset increases as W_0 is increased. This limiting rate of decrease for relative risk aversion depends on the riskless interest rate and other parameters, and thus is not as convenient to state, nor has the result generated much interest, perhaps because relative risk aversion for W is thought to not decrease very rapidly, if at all.

To summarize the portfolio findings, analysis of a simple portfolio model indicates that the slopes of the absolute and relative risk aversion measures partially determine how the level of initial wealth influences the allocation to the risky and riskless assets. If the allocation to both the risky and the riskless asset is to increase as initial wealth increases, then it must be that relative risk aversion neither increases nor decreases too rapidly. The first portion of this restriction is most easily stated by requiring that the measure of absolute risk aversion be decreasing.

Arrow (1965, 1971) also supports the assumption of increasing relative risk aversion for W by showing that if utility for W is to be bounded from below as W goes to zero, and bounded from above as W goes to infinity, then it must be that the relative risk aversion measure converges to a number less than or equal to one as W goes to zero, and converges to a number greater than or equal to one as W goes to infinity. He interprets this as support for increasing relative risk aversion for W because it requires that the relative risk aversion measure increase for at least some wealth levels, and prevents relative risk aversion from always declining. This argument linking boundedness of utility to the limiting values of relative risk aversion applies to any outcome variable and so the argument applies to the slope of relative risk aversion for all other outcome variables as well.

Arrow's argument based on the boundedness of utility also places particular significance on a particular magnitude of relative risk aversion, the value one. Arrow (1965, 1971) concludes that it is permissable to assume that relative risk aversion for W is increasing, although some fluctuation is permissable, and that if $R_u(W)$ is to be assumed to be a constant, then the appropriate value for that constant is one. This conclusion has been a starting point in attempts to determine the relative risk aversion measure for W in the forty or so years since Arrow made this claim.

Many of these findings of Arrow (1965, 1971) and Pratt (1964) have received considerable additional theoretical support in the forty years of research which has followed. The level of support for the various hypotheses does vary, however. A summary of our interpretation of these findings is given next, and a listing of a number of sources where comparative static theorems are demonstrated that lend support to these restrictions on the slope or magnitude of absolute and relative risk aversion for W is also presented.

There are literally hundreds of papers that make assumptions concerning the slope and/or magnitude of the absolute or relative risk aversion measure for wealth, and on the basis of those assumptions demonstrate comparative static findings within an economic model. That analysis provides additional information concerning the properties of these risk aversion measures for W. The literature concerning the demand for insurance, for instance, is an example of one such area where such research has been conducted, and a variety of assumptions concerning the risk aversion measures for W investigated.

In these economic models where wealth is the outcome variable, the analysis also addresses many comparative static questions in addition to the effect of an increase in initial wealth. For many of these questions, assumptions concerning the levels and slope of the risk aversion measures play a crucial role determining the direction of the comparative static effect of a parameter change. Within the portfolio model, for instance, one can ask how an improvement in the return to the risky asset affects the allocation of wealth to that asset. For this question and others like it, the answer depends on properties of the absolute and relative risk aversion measures for W. For example, Fishburn and Porter (1976) show that when relative risk aversion for W is less than or equal to one, $R_u(W) \leq 1$, then an investor would allocate more to the risky asset whenever the risky asset improves in a first degree stochastic dominant sense.

There are a large number of comparative static results of this sort that provide information and support for various assumptions concerning the magnitude and slope of absolute and relative risk aversion, many more than can be mentioned here. A listing of a sample of such papers follows. The list is partially organized by the economic decision model where the comparative static effect is determined.

Theoretical analysis supporting these hypotheses of Arrow (1965, 1971) and Pratt (1964) in more general portfolio setttings is provided by Cass and Stiglitz (1972), Fishburn and Porter (1976), Hadar and Seo (1990), and Meyer and Ormiston (1994). Analysis of insurance demand models for either co-insurance or deductible insurance, supports various assumptions concerning absolute and relative risk aversion. This analysis is found in work by Mossin (1968), Schlesinger (1981), Demers and Demers (1991), Meyer and Meyer (1998), Eeckhoudt et al. (1996), Eeckhoudt and Kimball (1992), Meyer and Meyer (1999), Eeckhoudt et al. (1997), and Briys et al. (1989).

Assumptions concerning risk aversion measures in expected utility models that are consistent with a mean-variance ranking function are investigated by Meyer (1987), and Eichner and Wagener (2004) and (2005). Finally, Hirshleifer and Riley (1992), Ichiishi (1997), and Mitchell (1994) examine these same measures in state preference and contingent claims models.

Several very broad findings are evident in this theoretical work where A-P wealth W is the outcome variable. These findings are as follows. First, the assumption of decreasing absolute risk for W has very strong support, and increasing absolute risk aversion is quite universally rejected. Second, increasing relative risk for W also is supported quite strongly, and the opposite property of decreasing relative risk aversion for W has little or no support in comparative static analysis. This lack of support for decreasing relative risk aversion may be because no restriction on the rate of decrease is typically imposed. When increasing relative risk aversion is assumed this assumption is almost always paired with the assumption of decreasing absolute risk aversion thereby restricting the rate of increase of relative risk aversion to be no faster than W. Finally, the assumption that the magnitude of relative risk aversion for A-P wealth is less than or equal to one has considerable support, while the opposite assumption of $R_u(W) \geq 1$ rarely plays a role in comparative static analysis.

3.2 Other measures of wealth

In many instances the definition or measure of wealth that is used in theoretical and especially in empirical analysis is not A-P wealth. Often the empirical wealth measure includes components of the decision maker's wealth even though those components cannot be reallocated to other assets or uses. Examples of such components of wealth may include the value of human capital, and the present discounted value of future transfer payments such as social security payments or other retirement benefits. In addition, there are other assets, such as owner occupied housing, whose value can only be reallocated to other assets at great cost and therefore it is questionable as to whether the value of these assets are or are not part of W. When components of wealth that cannot be reallocated or can only be reallocated at great cost are included when defining or measuring wealth, the relative risk aversion measure for the augmented wealth outcome variable differs in a predictable way from the relative risk aversion measure for A-P wealth.

Often relatively simple adjustments can be made so that relative risk aversion information for wealth, when wealth is not exactly W, can be used to infer the properties of the relative risk aversion measure for W itself. The process of adjusting for these added components depends on how the added component is related to W. Three separate simplifying assumptions are made so that the analysis relating the relative risk aversion measures for various measures of wealth is tractible. For each of the three cases, the assumption that is made implies that the function relating the new broader measure of wealth to A-P wealth is a linear function. This fact allows Theorem 2.4 to be used to indicate how the relative risk aversion for wealth is impacted by the inclusion of additional components.

When the definition or measure of wealth includes the value of assets that cannot be reallocated to other assets, it is denoted by W_+, indicating that components are added to A-P wealth. The case considered first is the situation where the value of these added components is a constant and does not vary with the random wealth W. An example of such a component of wealth might be the present value of an irreversible annuity. The present value of social security payments could also be another example of a component of wealth whose value is fixed and cannot be reallocated to other assets.[1]

When the value of a fixed component of wealth is added to W, the function relating W and W_+ is particularly simple and given by $W_+ = W + X$, where X is a constant greater than or equal to zero. These two outcome variables, W and W_+, are linearly related, and therefore the results presented in Theorem 2.4 apply. As a reminder, Theorem 2.4 indicates that the more inclusive outcome variable W_+, has a relative risk aversion measure with a larger magnitude than that for W, and the slope and elasticity or $R_v(W_+)$ tends to be smaller than that for $R_u(W)$. The exact relationship between the two risk aversion measures $R_u(W)$ and $R_v(W_+)$ is given in Theorem 2.4.[2]

One implication of this is that when a decision maker's relative risk aversion level for wealth is estimated using decisions involving an outcome variable that includes fixed components in addition to A-P wealth W, the process necessarily leads to a larger estimate for the magnitude and a reduced estimate for the slope and elasticity for relative risk aversion. When the value for X is known, the conversion of relative risk aversion information for utility function $v(W_+)$ so that it applies instead to $u(W)$ is an easy exercise using Theorem 2.4.

There are instances where the additional components of wealth whose value is included with the A-P measure are not constant, but are themselves random. This causes the analysis to become somewhat more complicated. Two extreme cases are considered. In the first case the added component, X, is assumed to be distributed independently from W. For the second case the other extreme is examined and the assumption is made that X and W are perfectly correlated. Each of

---

[1] In perfect capital markets one could always borrow against such expected future payments. The assumption here is that this is not possible.

[2] The measure of partial risk aversion is well suited to analysis of such situations, but is less well suited when representing the risk preferences of the decision maker. This is because the measure of partial risk changes with each change in the value for the fixed component of wealth, X.

these two extreme cases is sufficiently simple to allow relatively straight forward conclusions concerning the effect on the measure of relative risk aversion of wealth of including such a random component X with W.

When X is random and distributed independently from W, there is no fixed function describing the relationship between the two outcome variables W and W_+. As a consequence, the relationship between the utility functions $u(W)$ and $v(W_+)$ must be determined by another means. This issue has been dealt with in the literature under the subject of background risk or random initial wealth. Papers by Nachman (1982), and by Kihlstrom et al. (1981) are two of the important and early references on this topic. They begin their analysis by indicating that when X is distributed independently of W, then the utility function used to rank lotteries over W is related to that used to rank lotteries over W and X together by the equation $u(W) = E_X v(W + X)$.

Recall that $v(W + X)$ is the conditional utility function for W_+ conditioned on a fixed value for X. The relationship between the two utility functions, $u(W) = E_X v(W + X)$, is the expectation of these conditional utility functions. The right hand side of this expression is a convex combination of N-M utility functions. Pratt (1964) discusses the effect on absolute risk aversion of forming convex combinations of utility functions, and the methodology of his analysis is used here.

Given this relationship, $u(W) = E_X v(W + X)$, between the two utility functions, it appears that one can proceed to differentiate each side of this equation and determine the relationship between the risk aversion measures as before. Unfortunately, this approach rarely leads to a useful relationship between relative risk aversion measures because the expectation of a quotient is not the quotient of the expectations and other similar issues. Instead, some inferences concerning the impact of including a random but independently distributed X with W when measuring wealth are obtained by building on analysis presented by Pratt (1964).

Pratt's method of analysis is illustrated, and simultaneously extended to apply to relative risk aversion rather than absolute risk aversion, for the simple case where the random and independently distributed X can take on one of two possible values X_1 and X_2 with probabilities p_1 and p_2, respectively. Of course p_1 and p_2 sum to one.

For this two outcome case for independently distributed X, the expression $u(W) = E_X v(W + X)$ can be written out in full as

$$u(W) = p_1 \cdot v(W + X_1) + p_2 \cdot v(W + X_2)$$

The relationship between first derivatives and between the second derivatives of $u(W)$ and $v(W_+)$ take a similar form and are given by

$$u'(W) = p_1 \cdot v'(W + X_1) + p_2 \cdot v'(W + X_2)$$

and

$$u''(W) = p_1 \cdot v''(W + X_1) + p_2 \cdot v''(W + X_2)$$

Using these two functions and steps similar to those presented by Pratt (1964), the relationship between the relative risk aversion measure for $u(W)$, and the relative risk aversion measure for $v(W + X)$ is given by

$$R_u(W) = \frac{p_1 v'(W + X_1)}{[p_1 v'(W + X_1) + p_2 v'(W + X_2)]} R_v(W + X_1) \left[\frac{W}{(W + X_1)} \right]$$

$$+ \frac{p_2 v'(W + X_2)}{[p_1 v'(W + X_1) + p_2 v'(W + X_2)]} R_v(W + X_2) \left[\frac{W}{(W + X_2)} \right]$$

While this expression appears to be complicated, it is easier to understand and interpret when one examines each of the two lines separately. In the first line, the right hand term, $R_v(W + X_1) \left[\frac{W}{(W+X_1)} \right]$ is the exact expression giving the relationship between $R_u(W)$ and the relative risk aversion measure for the conditional utility function $v(W + X_1)$, when X takes on the fixed value X_1. This term expresses how the relative risk aversion measures $R_u(W)$ and $R_v(W + X_1)$ are related when X_1 is fixed. Similarly, in the second line, $R_v(W + X_2) \left[\frac{W}{(W+X_2)} \right]$ gives the relationship between $R_u(W)$ and $R_v(W + X_2)$ when X is fixed at $X = X_2$.

Now, observe that the left hand terms in each line are numbers that are positive and add to one. Thus, $R_u(W)$ is a convex combination of the already adjusted relative risk aversion measures for $v(W + X)$, where the adjustment is the one that is appropriate for the various possible fixed values for X.

The most immediate conclusion that one can draw is that the more inclusive outcome variable, W_+, even though the added component X

is random, has a utility function $v(W_+)$ with a larger magnitude of relative risk aversion than does $u(W)$. That is, even though X is assumed to be random, since X is positive, the relative risk aversion measure for $u(W)$ is smaller than that for $v(W + X)$ for each value for X, and this relationship carries through to the expectation as well. The relative risk aversion measure when X is random is an average of what occurs when X is fixed, and an average of something that is always larger must itself be larger.

Pratt (1964) also shows how slopes of absolute risk aversion measures are determined for convex combinations of utility functions. The steps used in that analysis can also be extended to show how the slopes of relative risk aversion measures are determined for convex combinations of utility functions. The process is more cumbersome and the details are not presented here even for the two outcome case. One can show, however, that the same general principle that applies to magnitudes also applies to slopes. The slope of $R_u(W)$ is a convex combination of the already adjusted slopes of $R_v(W + X)$ for each of the values for X. Thus, one can conclude that not only does $u(W)$ exhibit a smaller magnitude than $v(W_+)$, it also tends to have a larger slope and elasticity. Thus, the same conclusion that was obtained when X was fixed also applies when X is random and distributed independently from W. Including additional random components with W increases the magnitude of relative risk aversion and tends to decrease the slope and elasticity.

The precise impact on relative risk aversion of adding a random component X to W cannot easily be determined. That is, even though the direction of the impact of adding X whether it is fixed or random is much the same, the matter of adjusting is much more complicated when X is random than when X is fixed. One could simply fix X at its mean value and adjust as if X were constant. This leads to an adjustment in the appropriate direction, but the adjustment may be too large or too small.

The final and perhaps most interesting case of including an additional component of wealth with W is when that component, X, is random and not distributed independently from W. An example of such a component of wealth might be the value of human capital or a pension benefit, when the value of that human capital or pension benefit depends on the return to risky assets included with W, or is at least correlated with those returns. To simplify the analysis, the extreme case where X and W are not only correlated, but are perfectly correlated is considered.

When X and W are perfectly correlated, there exists a linear relationship, $X = a + \beta \cdot W$, between the two random components of wealth X and W. The sign of β determines whether the components of wealth are positively or negatively correlated, and the sign of the constant term a, determines whether the added component X is more or less risky than W. The riskiness of X and W is measured on a per unit basis by the coefficient of variation.

Consider first the case where $X = a + \beta \cdot W$ and $a > 0$ and $\beta > 0$. This case represents adding a component of wealth to W that is perfectly positively correlated with W, but has a smaller coefficient of variation since $a > 0$. When such an X is added to W, the expression for W_+ is given by $W_+ = W + X = W + (a + \beta \cdot W)$, or $W_+ = a + b \cdot W$, where b now equals $(\beta + 1)$. Since this is a linear relationship between the two different outcome variables, Theorem 2.4 can be used to determine the relationship between $R_u(W)$ and $R_v(W_+)$. With both a and b positive, the relative risk aversion measure for W_+ is larger than that for W, and the slope and elasticity of $R_v(W_+)$ tends to be smaller than that for $R_u(W)$.

The intuition behind this result is straightforward. The more comprehensively measured wealth variable W_+ is composed of two parts, and while each are risky, the W component is riskier than the X component. Since X is less risky than W, the result is that the relative risk aversion measure for W_+ adjusts in the same direction as would be the case when X is not only less risky than W, but not risky at all, that is, the fixed X case. Notice that the relative risk aversion measures would be the same if a were equal to zero so that X and W are perfectly correlated and equally risky.

As an example of the implication of this, consider an investor whose allocation between risky and riskless assets is observed, and the level of relative risk aversion is inferred from this allocation decision. For this investor, a lower magnitude is inferred when wealth is A-P wealth W

than when that same investor also is known to hold a less risky asset X which cannot be reallocated. Holding a less risky asset implies that one can take more risk with the wealth that can be reallocated, W, and not doing so must reflect a greater degree of risk aversion. Friend and Blume (1975) consider exactly this issue when they assume that the return to human capital is random, and that the value of human capital cannot be reallocated to other assets. The critical issue then is whether or not the return to human capital is less risky or more risky than the return to financial assets included with W.

When the additional component of wealth, X, is risker than W so that a is less than zero, the outcome of the analysis just conducted is reversed. W and W_+ are still linearly related and Theorem 2.4 can still be used, but the roles of W and W_+ are reversed. With X riskier than W so that $a < 0$, the more inclusively measured variable has a smaller magnitude of relative risk aversion and its slope and elasticity tend to be larger. Meyer and Meyer (2005b) in their review of Friend and Blume's (1975) inclusion of human capital with the wealth measure discuss this in considerable detail and use Friends and Blume's data to determine whether human capital, whose return is assumed to be risky, is more or less risky than the return on W.

In summary, when a decision maker includes components of wealth with A-P wealth and maximizes expected utility from wealth W_+, the measure of relative risk aversion that is estimated from that decision maker's choices is $R_v(W_+)$ not $R_u(W)$. Several different assumptions concerning how these added components might be related to W are suggested and used to determine how $R_v(W_+)$ and $R_u(W)$ are related. Whether X is fixed or random and independently distributed, as long as X is positive, the more comprehensive measure of wealth has the larger measure of relative risk aversion and tends to be more negatively sloped and has a smaller elasticity. When X is perfectly correlated with W, what is important to know is whether this added component is more or less risky than W. If less risky, the magnitude of relative risk aversion is increased and the slope and elasticity decreased. The opposite occurs when the added component is riskier than W.

The discussion so far deals with how to adjust for situations where the value of additional components of wealth are included with W so that the wealth measure is more inclusive than the A-P wealth measure. The opposite can also occur, components of wealth can be excluded from the A-P measure. Sometimes this may occur because the data do not include information on the value of certain assets. Hopefully, when this happens the magnitude of such an omission is small and would lead to only minor adjustments to the measure of relative risk aversion that is obtained. The procedure for converting information concerning relative risk aversion when W is undermeasured is similar to that just described and is discussed in more detail in Section 6.

3.3   Empirical evidence on relative risk aversion for wealth

In this section, the empirical evidence concerning relative risk aversion for wealth obtained from decision models where wealth is the outcome variable is reviewed. The majority of this evidence comes from examination of portfolio allocation decisions. Later on, relative risk aversion for other outcome variables including consumption, profit, and income is discussed. In that discussion, where ever possible, the evidence that is obtained for these other outcome variables is adjusted so that it also provides information concering relative risk aversion for wealth.

Quite surprisingly, there is very little direct empirical evidence concerning the magnitude of relative risk aversion for wealth. More evidence exists concerning how the magnitude of relative risk aversion for wealth changes with characteristics of the decision makers, such as their age, wealth level, income level, sex, marital status, retirement status etc. That evidence, however, is almost always presented without estimating a magnitude for relative risk aversion for wealth itself.

One of the very first papers to provide empirical information concerning relative risk aversion for wealth is that by Friend and Blume (1975). Friend and Blume use the proportion of wealth allocated to risky assets, α, as a measure of the reaction to risk by the decision maker. They use a quadratic approximation to the utility function for wealth so that the first order condition for maximizing expected utility is greatly simplified, and α can be explicitly solved for as a function of the first and second derivatives of utility. Using this approximation, they then show that α is the product of two terms. One term is the market price of risk in a mean-variance context, and the other is the inverse of the relative risk aversion measure for wealth evaluated at the initial wealth level. Friend and Blume assume that the outcome variable that enters the decision maker's utility function is after tax wealth, where taxes are imposed on investment gains and losses. Thus, a tax term also enters the expression for α.

Specifically, Friend and Blume (1975) show that for a quadratic approximation to utility, the optimal α is related to the market price for risk, $\frac{(\bar{r}-\rho)}{\sigma^2}$, the tax rate t, and the agent's relative risk aversion measure for after-tax wealth, $R_v(W_t)$, evaluated at the initial value for W. This relationship is given by

$$\alpha = \left[\frac{(\bar{r} - \rho)}{\sigma^2} \right] \cdot \left[\frac{1}{(1 - t) \cdot R_v(W_t)} \right]$$

In this expression $\bar{r}$ is the mean return on the risky asset, ρ is the return on the riskless asset, and σ^2 is the variance of the return to the risky asset.

Using data detailing the asset holdings of approximately 2100 households, Friend and Blume (1975) determine a value for α for each household. In doing this they must make a number of decisions concerning which assets are considered risky and which are considered riskless. They also estimate the market price of risk from historical data concerning returns to assets, and compute a tax rate for each household based on household income and other data.

Friend and Blume (1975) could combine this information to obtain an estimated value for $R_v(W_t)$ for each of these 2100 households. They do not do this. Instead, the 2100 households are grouped into five different wealth categories based on the level of household wealth. An average value for α is then calculated for each of these five wealth categories. The manner in which this average proportion of wealth allocated to the risky asset varies across the five wealth categories is investigated, and assumed to be the opposite of how the magnitude relative risk aversion varies by wealth category. The variation in relative risk aversion across wealth categories is interpreted as evidence concerning the slope of relative risk aversion for a representative decision maker. When α decreases as higher wealth categories are considered, then relative risk aversion is increasing for the representative decision maker, and vice versa.

Friend and Blume (1975) conduct their analysis using four different measures of wealth. None of these four measures is exactly A-P wealth because there are assets included with wealth whose value may not be reallocable. Also, their wealth measure differs from W because an after tax measure of wealth is used. As was just discussed, each of these variations from A-P wealth leads to increased estimates of the magnitude of relative risk aversion and decreased estimates of slope and elasticity. The four wealth measures used by Friend and Blume differ from one another by successively including additional components of wealth. Two different measures of the value of housing are sometimes included when measuring wealth, and also the value of human capital is sometimes included. Friend and Blume find that for some wealth measures, relative risk aversion for the representative decision maker increases slightly, while for others, it decreases slightly. No clear pattern of increasing or decreasing relative risk aversion for after tax wealth for a representative decision maker is obtained.

Meyer and Meyer (2005b) interpret Friend and Blume's (1975) findings by using their estimates for the average tax rate by wealth category, and the mean estimate of the market price of risk, to convert the average values for α for each wealth category into average values for relative risk aversion for after tax wealth for those categories. They report these values for three of the four wealth measures discussed by Friend and Blume. The first wealth measure does not include housing or human capital, the second includes the value of housing as measured by owner equity, and the third includes this measure of housing and also includes human capital as a fixed risky asset, whose return is correlated with W.

Using the procedures described in Section 3.2, Meyer and Meyer (2005b) not only calulate the values for $R_v(W_t)$, but also use the tax rate to convert these estimates of $R_v(W_t)$ to estimates for $R_u(W)$ assuming that W is the measure of wealth. The details of the conversions used are available in Meyer and Meyer. Broadly speaking, the estimated values for $R_u(W)$ fall in the range of 2 to 3. It should be noted that these reported values for relative risk aversion are estimates with the possibility of substantial error and perhaps this is why Friend and Blume (1975) do not report them. One source for this error is the ambiguity in the estimates for the market price of risk which range from 1.5 to 2.3, with a mean value of 2.0. In addition, by using the inverse of the average of α to determine the average value for $R_v(W_t)$, there is a downward bias. Jensen's inequality indicates that the inverse of the average is smaller than the average of inverse.

About the same time as the Friend and Blume (1975) analysis, Cohn et al. (1975) also present evidence concerning relative risk aversion for wealth based on portfolio allocation decisions made by risk averse investors. They use detailed asset holding information for 972 clients of a major brokerage firm who responded to a survey asking various questions including questions concerning asset holdings. Since their sample is restricted to clients of a brokerage firm, the holding of risky assets in their sample exceeds that observed by Friend and Blume in a random sampling of households. As in Friend and Blume, Cohn, Lewellen, Lease and Schlarbaum use the theoretical predictions from the single risky and riskless assets portfolio model. They determine whether the proportion of wealth held in the risky asset increases or decreases with the wealth of the investor, and interpret the finding that the proportion held in the risky asset increases as evidence of decreasing relative risk aversion for the representative decision maker.

Cohn et al. (1975) use two different classifications of assets into risky and riskless categories and also use two different measures of wealth. For all four of the resulting combinations, they find quite strong evidence that the proportion of wealth held in the form of risky assets increases with the wealth of the investor. This is interpreted as evidence of decreasing relative risk aversion for wealth for a representative investor. They do not provide information concerning the magnitude of relative risk aversion for wealth. They also provide extensive discussion concerning some of the difficulties encountered in performing the analysis.

More recently Blake (1996) uses similar portfolio composition information to determine the relative risk aversion characteristics for households in the United Kingdom. Like Friend and Blume (1975), Blake groups households into wealth categories and reports the average proportion of wealth held in the form of risky and riskless assets for each of six wealth categories. In his data set, the percentage of assets held in the form of risk free assets ranges from 86.5 for the lowest level of wealth to 29.4% for the highest, with this proportion allocated to the riskless asset decreasing uniformly as the level of wealth defining the category increases. These allocations to the risky and riskless assets are quite similar in range to those found by Friend and Blume who find that the average allocation to the riskless asset ranges from 81.4% to 5.6% as one moves from the lowest to the highest level category of wealth.

Blake (1996) uses a different but related model of investment choice. He assumes a mean-variance model of investor choice where the outcome variable is the rate of return on the investment. Blake assumes these outcome variables are normally distributed and that the investor is constant absolute risk averse. This allows expected utility to be written as a linear function of the mean and the variance of the rate of return from investment. Specifically, expected utility equals $\bar{r} + \frac{A}{2} \cdot \sigma^2$, where A now represents the absolute risk aversion for rate of return and $\bar{r}$ and σ^2 are the mean and variance of the rate of return on the investor's portfolio of assets not just the risky asset.

Blake (1996) spends a considerable of effort to estimate the parameters associated with the return on investment so that the efficient set of mean variance portfolios can be determined. Using the linear mean-variance utility function and the estimated efficient set in mean and variance of rate of return space, Blakes determines how the investor's allocation to the risky and riskless assets varies with risk aversion level. These values are converted to the relative risk aversion measure for the outcome variable rate of return. The reported values range from 0.476 to 0.0788, from the lowest wealth category to the highest, and the values for relative risk aversion for rate of return decrease uniformly as the wealth level defining the category is increased.

Blake's (1996) study is included in this section even though he does not use wealth as the outcome variable because his use of data on asset allocation is similar to that currently being discussed. To adjust to the reference relative risk aversion measure, $R_u(W)$, a function relating wealth W and rate of return r is needed. This function is given by the definitions of these two outcome variables and is $W = W_0(1 + r) = W_0 + W_0 \cdot r$. Notice in this case it is W that is written as a function of r, rather than the reverse, with the additive and multiplicative constants positive. Thus, $R_u(W)$ is larger than $R_v(r)$ and tends to be more negatively sloped. Using the analysis leading to Theorem 2.4, the implied relationship between the relative risk aversion measure for W and that r is

$$R_v(r) = \left[\frac{W_0 \cdot r}{W_0 + W_0 \cdot r}\right] \cdot R_u(W)$$

Meyer and Meyer (2005b) use Blake's reported mean value for r for each wealth category and the median value for the wealth category as W_0 to carry out the adjustment indicated. Since the factor $\left[\frac{W_0 \cdot r}{W_0 + W_0 \cdot r}\right]$ is generally quite a small number, the resulting risk aversion values for $u(W)$ are slightly higher, approximately 4, that those determined from the Friend and Blume (1975) analysis. Blake's analysis does give strong evidence of decreasing relative risk aversion both for $R_v(r)$ and for $R_u(W)$.

In the three studies just discussed, the decision maker's chosen allocation to the risky and riskless assets is assumed to be inversely related to the decision maker's relative risk aversion level for wealth. There are numerous reasons why the resulting relative risk aversion measure could differ from $R_u(W)$. The two just discussed are the inclusion of components of wealth not in W, and the uses of average of inverses as equal to inverses of averages. Another important issue is how the various assets are classified as risky or riskless. The various studies have sometimes classified bonds as riskless and other times as risky. Housing, when included as part of wealth is classified as risky by Friend and Blume (1975), but others argue that it should be considered riskless since it is the flow of services, which is arguably nonrandom, that represents the primary return from that investment. Two things must be kept in mind. First reclassifying an asset from risky to riskless, decreases the measured value for α, the proportion of wealth allocated to the riskly asset, and this can only lead to larger estimates for relative risk aversion.

Second, reclassification of assets from risky to riskless can also affect the estimate for the slope of relative risk aversion for wealth. This is because the asset that is reclassified can be a different proportion of wealth for the various wealth levels. Morin and Suarez (1983), using Canadian household portfolio data, illustrate how both the classification of housing and how the value of housing is measured affects α, and hence the estimate for relative risk aversion. They show that from the same data, when housing is excluded α rises and relative risk aversion falls with wealth, but when housing is considered a risky asset and measured by equity value the slope becomes nearly constant and when housing is measured by market value rather than equity value, α decreases with wealth implying increasing relative risk aversion. These findings result from the fact that housing is a much larger portion of wealth at low wealth levels than at high wealth levels.

A number of papers in the past thirty years have used this same two asset portfolio model and the theoretical findings relating the allocation to the risky and riskless assets to the level of relative risk aversion for wealth. Most of that effort has been devoted to determining how relative risk aversion for wealth varies with characteristics of the population. The level of relative risk aversion is rarely discussed in this analysis. Instead, α, the proportion of wealth allocated to the risk asset is treated as the dependent variable in an estimation model. From this work, information has been provided indicating how relative risk aversion for wealth, or actually the proportion of wealth allocated to risky assets, depends on age, sex, position in the life cycle, whether retired or not, and other characteristics of households. A partial listing of papers in this area includes Bellante and Saba (1986), Schooley and Worden (1996), Wang and Hanna (1997) and Bajtelsmit et al. (1999).

Riley and Chow (1992) use data from the Survey of Income and Program Participation (SIPP) and find that relative risk aversion is inversely related to age (up to age 65), education, and wealth and income. From responses to the 1989 Survey of Consumer Finances, Jianakoplos and Bernasek (1998) determine that single women exhibit more risk aversion in financial decision making than do single men. Sunden and Surette (1998) examine data from the 1992 and 1995 Surveys of Consumer Finances and find that investment decisions seem to depend on a combination of gender and marital status. Bellante and Green (2004) investigate relative risk aversion for wealth among the elderly and examine the effects on risk aversion due to age, race, gender, education, health status, and the number of children.

Other researchers have investigated the effects of demographic variables outside of the portfolio model setting. Halek and Eisenhauer (2001) estimate a model of life insurance demand using survey data from the 1992 University of Michigan Health and Retirement Study. They examine differences in relative risk aversion for wealth across groups based on age, gender, education, nationality, race, marital and parental status, and other factors.

Another study, which also uses the same simple portfolio model and the allocation to the risky asset as a measure of the reaction to risk, is by Dalal and Arshanapalli (1993). It differs from all others in that it does not use individual household portfolio allocation data but instead uses the aggregate allocation to risky and riskless assets in the United States as reported in Federal Reserve Board flow of funds data. Thus, the estimates provided are truly for a representative agent.

Using data from 1946 to 1985, Dalal and Arshanapalli (1993) measure the allocation to the riskless asset by the value of time and savings deposits and short term government securities. Total wealth is measured by household equity, and so the allocation to the risky assets is the difference between the two. From this data, first the hypotheses of constant absolute and constant relative risk aversion are tested, and the first hypothesis is rejected and the second is not. Then assuming constant relative risk aversion, Dalal and Arshanapalli are able to provides estimates for the level of this constant relative risk aversion. The value they present is $R_u(W) = 1.34$ with a standard error of 0.09. Dalal and Arshanapalli estimate relative risk aversion for wealth using a riskless asset measure that could under report the value of riskless assets. Also by using household equity as total wealth, they may also include more assets in the risky component of wealth than should be included with A-P wealth. This would tend to reduce estimates for relative risk aversion.

In summary, empirical research finds larger magnitudes and smaller slopes and elasticities for relative risk aversion for wealth than results from theoretical analysis concerning A-P wealth predict. This is consistent with empirical measures of wealth being broader and more inclusive that the theoretical concept A-P wealth. Even so, the relative risk aversion measure for wealth is typically quite small, perhaps as small as one or as large as four. In addition, the slope tends to be nearly flat when the magnitude is in the middle of this range, and tends to be rising when the estimated magnitude is small, and falling when the estimated magnitude is large.

4

Relative Risk Aversion for Consumption

In economic analysis under certainty, models of the decisions made by a consumer usually include more than one outcome variable. In the basic consumer model, for instance, the decision maker allocates income among two or more goods to maximize utility from those goods. The quantities of the various goods available for consumption are the outcome variables, and thus the utility function is a function with several arguments. Similarly, in a multi-period consumption setting, the decision maker chooses consumption quantities in the various time periods subject to a lifetime budget constraint. Again the utility function has several arguments.

When these models of consumption decisions, where the utility function has several arguments, are altered to include a source of randomness, it is possible to continue to assume than the utility function has more than one argument, and that expected utility is maximized. When one does this, however, risk aversion measures for a N-M utility function with more than one argument must be defined. As is stated at the outset, the measures of risk aversion provided by Arrow (1965, 1971) and Pratt (1964), and the discussion here, are for utility functions with just one argument or outcome variable. Thus, the first issue that must be dealt with in examining the relative risk aversion measure for consumption is to determine which assumption is to be used so that the utility function for consumption has just one argument.

Two approaches are taken in the literature. One is to assume an additive separable form for the multidimensional utility function with the same single dimensional utility function prevailing in each time period. The second approach focuses on risk aversion for one component of the multidimensional utility function holding the quantities of the other components fixed. This second approach can be used in contexts where the multiple arguments are not so related to one another such as when both the levels of health and of wealth comprise the outcome to the decision maker.

The economic model of consumption that is the focus here is one where the utility function from a vector of consumption outcome variables is additive separable, and the same utility function is used for each of the consumption outcomes. Most often this type of model is encountered in a multi-period consumption context, where utility from consumption in time periods 1 to n is assumed to take the form

$$U(C_1, \ldots, C_n) = \sum_{t=1}^{t=n} \beta^t v(C_t)$$

In this expression, $v(C_t)$ is utility from consumption in each time period, and the discounted sum of these utilities yields the total utility from the vector of consumption outcomes. Consumption in this model is the value of all goods consumed in the time period. A similar formulation for utility from consuming in different states of the world is also possible. In that case, the C_i represent the value of consumption in the various states of the world. Either of these two interpretations of the additive separable form for utility from consumption is consistent with the analysis conducted here.

Economic theory provides far fewer theorems concerning the risk aversion measures for $v(C)$ than are provided for $u(W)$. In part, this is because such theorems are more difficult to demonstrate. In many of the cases where such theorems do exist, the simplifying assumption that facilitates the demonstration of a theorem is that the number of time periods is limited to two. Furthermore, even with two time periods, it is often the case that assumptions are made so that only the consumption level in one of the two periods is random. Typically, in the first period the level of consumption is selected for certain, with the randomness in the decision model then implying that the level of second period consumption is random. For such models with just one random outcome variable, the analysis is simplified considerably.

For example, Rothchild and Stiglitz (1971) assume that a decision maker begins with wealth W_0 and chooses values for C_1 and C_2 to maximize $v(C_1) + \beta \cdot v(C_2)$. Consumption in period one, C_1, can be chosen for certain, and consumption in period two is then determined by the equation $C_2 = (W_0 - C_1) \cdot r$, where r is the random return earned from investing the wealth not consumed in the first period. Expected utility from consuming in the two time periods together is given by $v(C_1) + E[\beta \cdot v((W_0 - C_1) \cdot r)]$, and only the second component involves expected utility.

In this particular model of a consumption decision, Rothchild and Stiglitz (1971) show that the relative risk aversion measure for $v(C)$ is an important determinate of how the decision maker reacts to riskiness in the variable representing return to saved wealth. When relative risk aversion for C is less than one and increasing, an increase in the riskiness of r leads to an increase in C_1, which is equivalent to a reduction in saving for future consumption. The opposite occurs when $R_v(C)$ is greater than one and decreasing. For the case where $R_v(C)$ is constant, the reaction to an increase in the riskiness of return is determined completely by the magnitude of relative risk aversion. When $R_v(C)$ is constant and greater than one, then increased riskiness in the return to saving leads to an increase in saving, and when $R_v(C)$ is less than one, saving is decreased in response to such an increase in the riskiness of r.

Notice that in this model of Rothchild and Stiglitz (1971) where consumption occurs in just two time periods, consumption in period two, C_2, and final wealth W, are the same outcome variable and this is the only random outcome in the model. That is, in the last time period, the consumer chooses to consume the random final wealth. Since this last period is the only one involving randomness, the two utility functions, $u(W)$ and $v(C)$ are the same and there are no differences in risk attitudes toward consumption or wealth. Even though this model has two time periods, there is no difference between utility for the stock variable W or the flow variable C.

Sandmo (1968, 1970), Leland (1968) and others also make the assumption that just two time periods are being considered, and that all randomness occurs in the consumption level C_2. They do not, however, assume that the utility function is additive separable. Thus, utility is given by $U(C_1, C_2)$ and only C_2 is random. Because only one component of the utility function is random, the Arrow (1965, 1971) and Pratt (1964) definitions of absolute and relative risk aversion can be altered slightly focusing on the ratio of the second and first derivatives of $U(C_1, C_2)$ with respect to C_2. With this change in the Arrow and Pratt definitions, Leland and Sandmo are each able to demonstrate comparative static theorems in this model of consumption. The results they provide supports the assumption that absolute risk aversion for utility for C_2, $\frac{-U_{22}}{U_2}$, is a decreasing function of C_2.

In a state preference model of decisions under risk, the consumer chooses quantities of state contingent consumption $C_1, C_2, \ldots, C_n$ in each of the n states of the world. When the assumptions of expected utility are imposed on the utility function in this decision model, utility from consumption is given by

$$U(C_1, \ldots, C_n) = \sum_{i=1}^{i=n} p_i \cdot v(C_i)$$

In this formulation, C_i is consumption in state of the world i if that state occurs, and p_i is the probability of a particular state occurring. This expression is very similar in structure to that just presented for multi-period consumption under the assumpton of an additive separable utility function. The decision maker in this state preference model maximizes expected utility subject to the linear budget constraint $\pi_1 \cdot C_1 + \cdots + \pi_n \cdot C_n = W_0$, where π_i are the prices for state contingent consumption.

Hirshleifer and Riley (1992) present several comparative static theorems that help illustrate the meaning of various restrictions on relative or absolute risk aversion from consumption in this decision model. They are able to show, for instance, that under decreasing absolute risk aversion for $v(C)$, increases in W_0 lead to an increase in $|C_j - C_i|$ for all i

and j. The increased value for $|C_j - C_i|$ is interpreted as the consumer moving away from a constant level of consumption in all states of the world as absolute risk aversion decreases.

A similar result exists for relative risk aversion. When relative risk aversion is increasing, and C_j exceeds C_i, then increases in wealth lead to a relative decrease in expenditure on good j; that is $\frac{\pi_j \cdot C_j}{\pi_i \cdot C_i}$ falls. This is a movement in relative terms toward equal consumption in all states as relative risk aversion rises. For each of these results the converse is also the case.

Hirshleifer and Riley (1992) also present a result that allows one to interpret the magnitude of relative risk aversion for $v(C)$ in this state preference setting. They show that when $R_v(C) < 1$, then an increase in the price of a contingent claim leads to a smaller expenditure on that claim; that is, the own price elasticity of demand for a contingent claim is greater than one. The opposite is also true. When relative risk aversion for consumption is greater than one then the own price elasticity of demand for any claim is less than one.

In this expected utility version of a state preference model it is the case that when own price demand elasticity is greater than (less than) one, then all contingent claims are gross substitutes (complements). These three results concerning the magnitude and slope of risk aversion for contingent consumption allow one to interpret and perhaps test assumptions concerning the slopes and magnitudes for these risk aversion measures. The results do not argue strongly for any particular assumption concerning risk aversion for $v(C)$.

Empirical findings concerning risk aversion measures for consumption are also less numerous than for wealth. In addition,the findings that are available come from a much wider set of decision models and outcome variables than do those for wealth. There is no single decision model, with consumption as the outcome variable, that plays a role similar to that played by the portfolio model in demonstrating theorems or estimating parameters of risk aversion for wealth. Perhaps for this reason, the reported findings themselves are also less uniform than those for wealth.

One source of information concerning the risk taking propensities of consumers comes from the analysis of the responses of 11,707 consumers to a series of hypothetical questions concerning gambles over lifetime income conducted by Barsky et al. (1997) (BJKS). The questions examined are hypothetical and ask a consumer whether they would accept or reject a particular gamble that would either double family income for the consumer's lifetime, or reduce that income by a fixed percentage. Barsky, Juster, Kimball and Shapiro analyze the responses to such questions and interpret the change in lifetime income as a change in the level of consumption in each period for the consumer's lifetime.

BJKS (1997) assume the consumer exhibits constant relative risk aversion for the outcome variable, and based on the consumer's responses to the questions asked, are able to classify consumers into four categories according to their level of relative risk aversion for consumption. These four categories contain individual's whose relative risk aversion level falls in the intervals $[0, 1]$, $[1, 2]$, $[2, 3.76]$ and $[3.76, \infty)$, respectively. Since risk tolerance aggregates linearly, BJKS convert this information concerning relative risk aversion to its inverse, risk tolerance. These same four categories contain individuals whose risk tolerance measure falls in the intervals $[1, \infty)$, $[.5, 1]$, $[.27, 0.5]$ and $[0, 0.27]$, respectively.

BJKS's (1997) primary focus is on how risk tolerance and hence relative risk aversion varies with a variety of characteristics of the population. To examine for increasing or decreasing risk tolerance and hence decreasing or increasing relative risk aversion, how risk tolerance varies with the respondent's current income and current wealth is examined. BJKS find that the variation in risk tolerance across groups defined by either current wealth or income is quite small, ranging from 0.2318 to 0.2601 for current wealth, and from 0.2310 to 0.2556 for current income. Neither of the patterns of variation is strictly increasing or decreasing and thus little evidence supporting increasing or decreasing risk tolerance or relative risk aversion for consumption is found.

To convert the BJKS (1997) estimates of average level of risk tolerance to estimates of the magnitude of relative risk aversion involves inverting. In addition, one must also take into account the fact that the average of the inverse exceeds the inverse of the average. In their table 1, BJKS report both average risk tolerances and average relative risk aversion levels for four groups of consumers. Based on the relationship between the inverse of the average and the average of the inverse reported in that table, it appears that in this particular data, the average of the inverse is approximately double the inverse of the average.

Assuming that the average of the inverse is precisely double the inverse of the average, the level of relative risk aversion found by BJKS (1997) is approximately $(1/.25)(2) = 8$. At a minimum the level is 4, and it could be even larger than 8. In one of their many qualifying remarks BJKS indicate that this level of relative risk aversion may be biased upward due to a status quo bias in the formulation of the questions asked. In the survey, consumers were asked about changing from their current job, to a new job with either double the current income or a fixed percentage reduction in current income. Thus, rejecting such a lottery, interpreted by BJKS as evidence of risk aversion, can be simply rejecting change. BJKS do find high levels of relative risk aversion for an outcome variable referred to as lifetime consumption.

Eeckhoudt and Hammitt (2001) present a simple model relating the consumption/wealth elasticity of the value of statistical life (VSL) to the magnitude of relative risk aversion for consumption/wealth evaluated at the level that occurs when the decision maker is alive. Since there is only one time period, wealth and consumption are the same outcome variable. Kaplow (2005) presents similar analysis and indicates that this level of relative risk aversion for consumption must be smaller than the elasticity of VSL. He then points out that the results presented by Viscusi and Aldy (2003) indicate that the consensus estimate of the elasticity of VSL is between 0.5 and 0.6, implying very low levels of relative risk aversion for consumption. Kaplow interprets this as *a previously unrecognized (additional) anomaly concerning individual's risk-taking behavior in different market settings.*

An alternate interpretation involves recognizing that the relative risk aversion measure in the Kaplow (2005) analysis is evaluated at the highest of the two possible consumption levels in the gamble over consumption that the decision maker is evaluating. These two possible levels for consumption are $C = 0$ and the higher level is approximately $C = 6$ million dollars. By evaluating the relative risk aversion measure only at the highest level for C, any effects from decreasing relative risk aversion for C are missed. Requiring or finding that relative risk aversion is very low at this highest consumption level does not reject larger values for relative risk aversion at lower consumption levels if relative risk aversion is a decreasing function of consumption.

In research related to the equity premium puzzle, Constantinides (1990) estimates and calibrates a model where utility from current consumption depends in part on past levels of consumption. In this multiperiod consumption setting, with additive separable utility, the utility for consumption has associated with it a value function for wealth. While Constantinides main purpose is not the estimation of relative risk aversion levels for either the utility function for consumption or for the value function for wealth, he does report these estimates. Constantinides finds that the predictions from the model can match historical data involving returns on risky and riskless assets and time patterns of consumption, when utility from consumption takes on the following functional form.

$$v(C) = \frac{(C - X)^{(1-\alpha)}}{(1 - \alpha)}$$

The relative risk aversion measure for this utility function is $R_v(C) = \frac{\alpha C}{(C-X)}$. This relative risk aversion measure is decreasing in C whenever X is greater than zero.

Constantinides (1990) estimates that at the mean value for C, the value for X is approximately 0.8C. Thus, at this mean value the magnitude of relative risk aversion is 5α. He reports five different calibrations of the habit formation process that can match the historical data. For these five different sets of parameter values, $R_v(C)$ at the median level of consumption range from 11.6 to 15.7. Of course, with this form for $v(C)$, the slope of relative risk aversion is quite negative. The levels of relative risk aversion for value function for wealth that Constantinides reports range from 7.03 down to 2.78. An explanation of why these values for $R_u(W)$ are much lower than those for $R_v(C)$ is given shortly.

Ogaki and Zhang (2001) use food consumption as the outcome variable, and estimate the slope of relative risk aversion for food consumption using data concerning decisions made by households in Pakistan and India. They do not estimate the magnitude of this relative risk aversion measure. Ogaki and Zhang find strong evidence that relative risk aversion for food consumption is decreasing. A more detailed discussion of the evidence concerning relative risk aversion for consumption provided by each of the three papers just reviewed is available in Meyer and Meyer (2005b).

As mentioned by BJKS (1997), a large number of studies attempting to explain the pricing of risky assets in the United States and elsewhere, have determined that relative risk aversion for consumption must be very large with estimates ranging from 10 to more than 100 in some instances. In these studies, the form for the utility function for consumption is almost always assumed to be one where the relative risk aversion measure for consumption is constant. As the Constantinides (1990) work shows, these levels of relative risk aversion can be greatly reduced when the slope of relative risk aversion is allowed to be negative instead. The discussion that follows is an attempt to clarify why this the case. The discussion draws heavily on two recently published papers by Meyer and Meyer (2005a,b).

In multi-period consumption models with additive separable utility for consumption, the one dimensional utility function for consumption in each period is related, using the envelope theorem, to the indirect utility function for wealth. Wealth in these models is a stock variable that can be carried across time periods and used to smooth the patterns of consumption over time. In a few special cases of this multi-period consumption model, the relationship between the utility functions for wealth and consumption can be determined explicitly.

Meyer and Meyer (2005a), for instance, show that when utility for consumption takes the form $v(C) = \frac{(C-X)^{(1-\alpha)}}{(1-\alpha)}$, then the value function $u(W)$ takes the form $u(W) = \frac{(W)^{(1-\alpha)}}{(1-\alpha)}$. This is the constant relative risk averse form for $u(W)$ and a decreasing relative risk averse form for $v(C)$. Using a similar model, Kimball and Mankiw (1989) show that when utility from consumption in each period takes the constant absolute risk averse form, $v(C) = -e^{-\lambda C}$, then optimal consumption is again a linear function of wealth, and the value function for utility function for wealth takes the form $u(W) = -e^{-\gamma W}$. This is also a constant absolute risk averse form for utility for wealth with a different absolute risk aversion parameter that for the associated utility function for consumption (Example 2.2).

In most other instances, with different functional forms for $v(C)$ and different modeling assumptions, finding the relationship between C and W and finding the specific $u(W)$ associated with a particular $v(C)$ is not possible. It is always the case, however, that when the decision maker maximizes expected utility from this additive separable form for utility from consumption, the marginal utility from an additional unit of wealth equals the marginal utility from an additional unit of consumption purchased with that wealth. The envelope theorem guarantees this.

The equation $v'(C) = u'(W)$ gives a relationship between the two utility functions that allows the functions relating the absolute and relative risk aversions measures for these two utility functions to be obtained by direct calculation. These relationships are given by

$$A_u(W) = A_v(C)\left[\frac{dC}{dW}\right]$$

and

$$R_u(W) = R_v(C)\left[\frac{dC}{dW}\right]\left[\frac{W}{C}\right]$$

One can use these expressions to convert measures of absolute or relative risk aversion for the one utility function to those for the other using information concerning the marginal propensity to consume and the magnitudes of consumption and wealth.

Because both Kimball and Mankiw (1989) and Meyer and Meyer (2005a) find that optimal consumption is a linear function of wealth, and for reasons of simplicity, the assumption is made here that the function relating consumption to A-P wealth is given by $C = a + b \cdot W$. In this expression W is A-P wealth, and C is a full or complete measure of consumption in each time period in a multiperiod setting. With this linear relationship assumption, the relationships between risk aversion measures for $u(W)$ and $v(C)$ reduce to

$$A_u(W) = A_v(C)[b]$$

and

$$R_u(W) = R_v(C) \left[\frac{b \cdot W}{C}\right] = R_v(C) \left[\frac{b \cdot W}{a + b \cdot W}\right]$$

Using aggregate consumption and wealth data and the estimate for X provided by Constantinides (1990) and other sources, Meyer and Meyer (2005b) conclude that the magnitude of the constant coefficient a in this linear function is at least 0.8 W at the mean value for W, and thus at the mean value for W, the relative risk aversion measure for $v(C)$ is five times larger than that for $u(W)$. Furthermore, the slope and elasticity of the relative risk aversion measure for $v(C)$ tend to be smaller than those for $u(W)$. In fact, a constant relative risk aversion measure for $u(W)$ requires severely decreasing relative risk aversion for consumption.

In summary, there is far less theoretical or empirical evidence concerning relative risk aversion for consumption than for wealth. At first glance, the evidence concerning $R_v(C)$ appears to contradict that for $R_u(W)$. This is not the case, however, when the marginal propensity to consume from wealth is small. Small and relatively constant values for relative risk aversion for wealth are consistent with high and severely declining measures of relative risk aversion for consumption.

5

Relative Risk Aversion for Profit

A considerable amount of theoretical research has been conducted for economic models where the decision maker maximizes expected utility from an outcome variable referred to as profit. In part this is because the theory of the firm is an important component of microeconomic theory, but this also is because this is an outcome variable of one dimension, and therefore extending models without randomness to models which include randomness is straightforward. Even with randomness, the same outcome variable can be used, and the argument of the N-M utility function is such that the definitions of risk aversion provided by Arrow (1965, 1971) and Pratt (1964) can be employed without modification.

Economic profit is defined to be the difference between the revenues received from producing and selling goods and the costs incurred in doing so. It is a flow variable, although most models where firms maximize profit do not involve multiple time periods so in those models this distinction is not important. As economists we have all reminded our students that the revenues and costs are economic revenues and economic costs, and that these concepts are not necessarily the same as the terms are used in everyday language or as defined by an accountant.

This point is important to keep in mind as the measures of profit used in empirical work are discussed.

One of the more basic theoretical models where the expected utility from economic profit is maximized is that presented by Sandmo (1971). He assumes that a competitive firm chooses its output level to maximize the expected utility from profit and assumes that output price is a nonnegative random variable and taken as given by the firm. In that model, the notation used is $\pi = p \cdot x - c(x) - B$, where π represents profit, p is the random price of the output, x is the output level, $c(x)$ is the variable cost function and B is interpreted as the fixed component of costs.

When firms maximize the expected utility from profit where $\pi = p \cdot x - c(x) - B$, certain risk aversion properties for the utility function $v(\pi)$ have more support than do others. For instance, the assumption that absolute risk aversion for profit, $A_v(\pi)$, is decreasing, implies that a risk averse firm reacts to an increase in fixed costs by reducing the output level. That same assumption concerning absolute risk aversion also implies that when the random output price is increased by adding a positive constant to it, then the decreasing absolute risk averse firm reacts to this increase in price by increasing the amount produced. Sandmo (1971) demonstrates each of these results and indicates that both seem to be natural reactions for a risk averse firm. In addition, the opposite reaction occurs when the firm is assumed to display increasing absolute risk aversion for profit. These results are viewed as providing support for the assumption of decreasing absolute risk aversion when the outcome variable is profit, and the results lead to the rejection of the assumption of increasing absolute risk aversion for profit.

There are not many theorems concerning maximization of expected utility from economic profit where assumptions concerning relative risk aversion for profit play an important role. Those results that do exist require careful interpretation since economic profit can take on both positive and negative values. Sandmo (1971), for instance, shows that when profit is taxed at a fixed rate, including tax rebates when profit is negative, then an increase in the tax rate increases output level under increasing relative risk aversion for profit while the opposite occurs under decreasing relative risk aversion. Since the sign of the relative risk aversion measure changes as profit passes through zero, and is zero when profit equals zero, these are very restrictive assumptions concerning the risk taking propensity of the firm. The assumption of constant relative risk aversion only includes the case of relative risk aversion equals zero.

Baron (1970) discusses a model quite similar to that of Sandmo and provides an interesting alternate interpretation for the fixed component in the expression defining profit. This interpretation allows one to avoid the difficulties associated with relative risk aversion measures for negative values for profit. Baron assumes that profit is a flow that is added to the firm's existing wealth, so that B represents not only the fixed cost the firm incurs, but also represents the initial wealth that the firm has at the beginning of the period. That is, $B = TFC - W_0$, where TFC is fixed cost, and W_0 is the initial wealth of the firm. When the constant term B is interpreted in this way, B is likely to be negative rather than positive, and the assumption that outcome variable is always positive is more likely to be an acceptable one. The sign of B seems to not affect the majority of the results that are presented by either Baron or Sandmo. With this interpretation of the constant term B, the variable referred to as profit in such models with just one time period is the same as final wealth. The production and selling activities of the firm are simply ways to add to the existing wealth of the firm.

More recently, Hadar and Seo (1993) show that if $R_v(\pi)$ is less than one, then a first degree stochastic dominant improvement in output price leads to an increase in output level. When $R_v(\pi)$ is greater than one, such an improvement in output price can lead to either an increase or a decrease in the output level. Hadar and Seo also show that an increase in the riskiness of output price leads to a reduction in the chosen output level when $R_v(\pi)$ is less than one and increasing. These findings are interpreted as providing modest support for increasing relative risk aversion for profit and for a magnitude of relative risk aversion that is less than one. Again the possibility that profit is negative must be taken into account in interpreting these results.

Virtually all empirical work dealing with relative risk aversion for profit concerns the risk taking characteristics of agricultural producers. In much of the empirical analysis the estimation of a level or slope for relative or absolute risk aversion is only a portion of the estimation being conducted, with production function and technology parameters also receiving considerable attention in the formulation of the estimation model. The term profit is used to describe the outcome variable in these studies but the outcome variables themselves vary considerably across the various studies. In most cases profit is actually net revenue or net income because a number of significant components of costs are not included in the analysis because of data limitations.

A relatively recent and well documented study of the choices made by agricultural producers is that by Saha, Shumway and Talpaz (1994) (SST). In their analysis, the agricultural producers, fifteen Kansas wheat farmers, are observed to chose input quantities, and the assumption is made that these quantities are chosen to maximize expected utility from an outcome variable that SST refer as wealth. Their outcome variable is not wealth as the term is used here, nor is it profit. The outcome variable employed by SST consists of the sum of farm revenue and off-farm income, and subtracted from this are the costs of farm production. No labor costs are included because of data limitations. In their sample, the average farm revenue is approximately 72% of total revenue with off-farm income contributing the remaining 28%. Agricultural production costs are large, and are approximately 86% of agricultural revenue. For the average decision maker, more net income comes from off-farm sources than from agricultural production. In the SST data there is no A-P wealth variable. We interpret their outcome variable as net income for the farm family rather than economic profit.

For this outcome variable, SST (1994) jointly estimate production parameters and parameters describing the risk taking propensities of the decision maker. They use a flexible functional form for the utility function so that the magnitudes and the slopes of absolute and relative risk aversion are unrestricted. This flexible form allows testing for decreasing or increasing absolute or relative risk aversion, as well as providing evidence concerning the magnitudes of these risk aversion measures. SST indicate that the data supports the assumptions of decreasing absolute risk aversion and increasing relative risk aversion for this outcome variable. They also find that the magnitude of relative risk aversion at the mean level of the outcome variable is between 3.8

and 5.4 depending on the sample used in the estimation. Interpretation of these findings and those that follow is deferred to the end of the section.

Chavas and Holt (1996) use aggregate data for the farm sector rather than data concerning an individual producer. They examine the decision to allocate farm land in a particular region of the country to the production of corn or the production of soybeans. The production of each of these commodities is assumed to produce a net return per acre which is random. The allocation decision and how it changes over time with changes in the riskiness of the net income variables is used to estimate the risk taking characteristics of a representative agricultural producer.

In the Chavas and Holt (1996) analysis, the decision maker chooses to allocate farm land to either corn or soybean production. The price and quantity produced per acre for each commodity are random variables, while the cost of production per acre is a known constant. The allocation decision is assumed to be made to maximize expected utility from net income from the land available for production. This outcome variable is the economic profit from the land that is available as long as all economic costs and revenues are included in the calculation. Chavas and Holt use a flexible form for the utility function of the decision maker. Because profit can be negative, Chavas and Holt focus on the absolute risk aversion measure. They find that the data supports the restriction that absolute risk aversion is decreasing. Chavas and Holt also report an estimated value for relative risk aversion for profit of approximately six at the mean level of profit. The mean level of profit is positive.

In a followup paper to SST (1994), Saha (1997) proposes a new estimation technique and implements the technique using the same data set that is analyzed in SST. This new method jointly estimates the level of risk aversion, the structure of risk preferences, and the production technology in a nonlinear mean-standard deviation model. The mean-standard deviation framework corrects a weakness in expo-power utility function used in the earlier SST study which biases the findings toward increasing relative risk aversion. The utility function used by Saha in a mean-standard deviation formulation is $U(M,S) = M^a - S^b$, where

M and S are the mean and standard deviation of the outcome variable referred to here as net farm family income.

This flexible utility form allows all possible combinations of the slope possibilities for absolute and relative risk aversion. Using the data concerning the decisions made by the same fifteen Kansas wheat farmers, Saha (1997) finds evidence of risk aversion and decreasing absolute risk aversion. Evidence concerning the slope of relative risk aversion is mixed and depends on the size of the producer. No evidence of decreasing relative risk aversion for this outcome variable is found, and some groups display constant while others display increasing relative risk aversion.

A study by Lence (2000) focuses on simultaneously estimating farmers' time preferences and risk attitudes in an intertemporal consumption model. He estimates parameters in a multi-period generalized expected utility model using data on aggregate consumption and asset returns. By using a generalized expected utility model, the rate of time preference and elasticity of intertemporal substitution can be separated from the risk preferences of the decision maker. He finds that the more general model fits the data better than the traditional model.

The outcome variable in the utility function is consumption where consumption is measured by real withdrawals per farm operator. Components of this variable include gross cash income, value of home consumption, and off-farm income. The basic data come from the farm sector's income statements and balance sheets published by the US Department of Agriculture. Data spans the time period from 1936 to 1994. Given the usage of aggregate versus individual farm level data, the estimates obtained are interpreted as pertaining to a representative agent of the farm sector.

A point estimate of the coefficient of relative risk aversion was obtained by performing a second-order Taylor series approximation. Lence (2000) estimates a magnitude of relative risk aversion equal to 1.136 with a 95% confidence interval of (1.061, 1.211). When the sample is divided into two time periods, 1936–64 and 1966–94, results show that relative risk aversion has decreased over time. The estimated value for relative risk aversion for the first time period was 2.51, while that for the second period was 1.13. It is unclear whether the outcome variable in this analysis is more like net income, or like consumption as reviewed in Section 4.

Bontems and Thomas (2000) (BT) address the issue of splitting nitrogen applications as a risk reduction strategy by modeling agricultural crop production as a multistage process. The first application of fertilizer (nitrogen) is applied at or before planting and then a second application (sidedressing) is made during growth of the crop prior to harvest. BT jointly estimate production and technology parameters along with risk aversion parameters for the decision maker. The argument of the utility function is referred to as profit. Several components of the cost of production are omitted in the profit calculation so net income is likely a better term. Profit or net income per acre is the difference between revenue and the costs of the two nitrogen applications and the cost of some other predetermined input quantities. For the costs of the predetermined inputs, only the labor used in fertilizer applications is included. Data is collected from several USDA sources.

BT (2000) use a constant relative risk averse form for the utility function which requires the outcome variable to always be positive. They estimate that the level of relative risk aversion is 3.7. They use corn production and fertilization data from the Midwest from 1990–92. The estimated level of relative risk aversion of 3.7 is found to be significantly different from zero at the 5% level of significance.

Kumbhakar (2002) focuses on the joint estimation of risk preferences, production parameters and risk levels, and technical inefficiency. The risk preference function is decomposed into two parts, one associated with production risk and the other with technical inefficiency. Both additive and multiplicative models are estimated. A main contribution of the paper is the manner in which the production portion of the problem is estimated.

Data on Norwegian salmon farms is used for estimation purposes. The outcome variable in the utility function is referred to as profit. Profit is defined to be the revenues from salmon production including the value of unsold salmon at year end minus the costs of variable inputs. No data on existing wealth or income from other sources is used. Kumbhakar (2002) reports that the evidence supports the assumption of decreasing absolute risk aversion. The coefficient of relative risk aversion, calculated by using the mean level of profit level, was very low and equal to 0.051. This could be because salmon production may not be the main production activity of the decision maker.

To interpret this and similiar information concerning relative and absolute risk aversion for outcome variables referred to as profit or net income, a framework connecting these outcome variables to the outcome variables that have been already discussed is useful. The discussion that follows provides such a framework by drawing on and extending the earlier analysis where a function relating wealth and consumption is determined.

The first thing to recognize is that the outcome variable referred to as profit or net income is more similar to consumption than wealth. Profit or net income is a flow rather than a stock variable. As was mentioned in the section discussing utility for consumption, for models with only one period, this distinction is of little consequence. In fact, Baron's (1970) interpretation of the fixed term B, is a one period model, and then profit and wealth are equivalent. Such a formulation misses an essential aspect of profit or net income as an outcome variable, just as a similar one or two period formulation of a model of consumption misses an important aspect of consumption as an outcome variable.

To examine profit or net income in a broader context, consider the following model where wealth, consumption and net income are each variables within the model, and these three variables are related to one another by the function giving optimal consumption as a function of wealth and net income. The multi-period consumption models of Kimball and Mankiw (1989) and Meyer and Meyer (2005a) are adapted slightly to formulate such a model. Recall that in these models, the consumer chooses consumption in each time period to maximize expected utility from consumption, and the consumption level selected depends on the wealth that is saved from previous periods, and other variables. One of these other variables is the level of income that occurs in each period.

Kimball and Mankiw (1989) include both wealth and income in their model. Wealth is a stock variable and return on wealth is not random. Income, on the other hand, is recurring, with the amount in each period being a random variable. K-M have in mind income from employment, but this income variable can also be interpreted as net income from agricultural production. In this setting, assuming a constant absolute risk averse utility function for consumption, Kimball and Mankiw are able to solve for the optimal level of consumption. As was noted earlier, this optimal consumption level of consumption is a linear function of wealth and this provides a form for the relationship between consumption and wealth. What is important to note now, however, is that optimal consumption is also a linear function of income. The additive constant term in the linear function relating consumption to wealth is the income variable. Thus, not only is optimal consumption a linear function of wealth, it is also a linear function of income received in each period.

The similar multi-period consumption model of Meyer and Meyer (2005a) also generates this same result. In that model it is assumed that a decision maker chooses consumption in each period to maximize expected utility from consumption. Utility for consumption is assumed to take the decreasing relative risk averse form mentioned earlier (Example 2.3). Also, in the M-M formulation the recurring income flow is not stochastic, but is a fixed amount in each time period. In the M-M model the return to wealth is random. M-M are able to explicitly derive the optimal consumption function, and this function is linear in wealth and also linear in the non random income variable. On the basis of these two models with explicit solutions for optimal consumption, the simplifying assumption that is made here is that outcome variables consumption, income and wealth are related by the equation $C = Y + b \cdot W$, where Y represents income. Consumption is a linear function of wealth, but it is also a linear function of the recurring income that is available in each time period.

This function, linking the three outcome variables, can be used to determine a relationship between the relative risk aversion measures for any pair of outcome variables assuming that the third outcome variable is held fixed. This was done earlier when deriving the relationship between the relative risk aversion measures for outcome variables C and W. In the course of deriving this relationship, it was assumed that Y was fixed and simply denoted as the constant term a in the linear function relating C and W. Thus, the constant a in the equation

$$R_u(W) = R_v(C) \left[\frac{b \cdot W}{C} \right] = R_v(C) \left[\frac{b \cdot W}{a + b \cdot W} \right]$$

can now be interpreted as the fixed level of income that recurs each period from sources other than wealth.

Since the focus in this section is on profit or net income which is denoted Y, a procedure that is similar can be used to relate the relative risk aversion measure for Y to that for C. Assume now that the portion of consumption paid for from wealth is fixed so that $C = (b \cdot W) + Y$, where $(b \cdot W)$ is the constant term in this linear function. This is a linear relationship between the outcome variables C and Y with both constants in the linear function being positive. Thus, the derivations leading to Theorem 2.4, and Theorem 2.4 itself, apply. This analysis implies that the relationship between the relative risk aversion measures for Y and C is given by

$$R_{\tilde{v}}(Y) = R_v(C) \left[\frac{Y}{C} \right] = R_v(C) \left[\frac{Y}{b \cdot W + Y} \right]$$

In this expression, the utility function for outcome variable Y is $\tilde{v}(Y)$ and its relative risk aversion measure is $R_{\tilde{v}}(Y)$.

This relationship indicates that relative risk aversion for net income should always be less than that for consumption and how much less depends on the proportion of consumption financed through net income and the proportion financed through return on wealth. For the agricultural producers whose risk preferences are estimated in the studies that were reviewed here, net income is larger than return from wealth, and therefore a finding that relative risk aversion for profit or net income is between that for wealth and consumption but closer to that for consumption is a consistent finding.

6

Relative Risk Aversion for Other Outcome Variables

6.1 Omitted variables discussion

There are a number of papers reporting information concerning the levels and slopes of risk aversion for outcome variables that are a component of, but not all of, one of the outcome variables discussed so far. These random payoffs received by the decision maker result from the choices of the decision maker. These payoff amounts are viewed as components of a larger outcome variable such as wealth or consumption or net income. Sometimes the payoffs are only a small component of the larger outcome variable, and often there is little or no information concerning the magnitude of the missing components. Outcome variables with this characteristic are referred to here as payoffs, and the symbol used to represent the size of the payoff is X.

As an example of a setting where the outcome variable is a payoff, consider the evaluation of the results of an experiment where a decision maker chooses between a pair of gambles A and B. For gamble A there is a 50–50 chance of receiving a payoff equal to USD0 or USD20. For gamble B there is a 50–50 chance of receiving payoffs equal to either USD5 or USD13. It is typical and natural in this setting to focus on an outcome variable X whose possible values include the payoffs of 0, 5,

13 or 20. This is the case even though it is recognized that the decision maker likely has other wealth or income, to which the payoff from the experiment is to be added. When A-P wealth is this outcome variable to which the payoff is added, then $W = W_0 + X$, where W_0 denotes A-P wealth before the random payoff X is received and added to it.

The assumption is made that the utility from a payoff X is determined by the utility from W which includes the payoff X. That is, the payoff outcome variable X is a component of W so that $W = W_0 + X$ and thus $u(W) = u(W_0 + X) = v(X)$ defines the relationship between utility function $u(W)$ and $v(X)$. Although the discussion presented here is for the relationship between the risk aversion measures for payoff X and for A-P wealth W, the exact same relationships between risk aversion measures hold when any one of the three main outcome variables discussed in Sections 3, 4 and 5 is considered. That is, W can be replaced by C or by Y, and the relationships between the risk aversion measure for X and for C or Y is the same as that presented here for X and W.

The analysis leading to the relationship between the risk aversion measures for X and for W is very similar to that presented in Section 3.2 where the effect on risk aversion measures of adding components to W is determined. Now, however, it is the case that components are added to X rather than W, or put differently, X is obtained from W by omitting components from W rather than adding components to it. This reversal of the roles of X and W, leads to an exact reversal of the general findings presented in Section 3.2.

When $X = W - W_0$, one can consider several cases. The two considered here are where the omitted component, W_0, is fixed, and the case where W_0 is random and distributed independently from X. These two cases each lead to relationships between the risk aversion measures for X and W that are symmetric to those reported in Section 3.2 and because of this similarity, far less detail is provided.

Suppose that the payoff being considered is such that the omitted components of A-P wealth are fixed, so that $W = W_0 + X$ or $X = W - W_0$, where W_0 is a constant greater than or equal to zero. These two outcome variables, W and X are linearly related, and therefore analysis leading to Theorem 2.4 and the the results presented there apply. This analysis implies that the relationship between $R_v(X)$ and $R_u(W)$ is given by

$$R_v(X) = R_u(W) \left[\frac{W - W_0}{W}\right] = R_u(W) \left[\frac{X}{W}\right]$$

From this it is easily observed that the more inclusive outcome variable W, has a larger magnitude of relative risk aversion than does the payoff variable X. This is property (a) in Theorem 2.4. Also, the larger the payoff relative to the omitted component, the larger the magnitude of relative risk aversion for the payoff.

It is also the case that properties (b) (c) and (d) of Theorem 2.4 give the relationship between the slopes and elasticities of these two relative risk aversion measures. Loosely speaking, $R_u(W)$ has a smaller slope and elasticity when evaluated at the corresponding values for W and X than does $R_v(X)$. Thus, estimation of a decision maker's relative risk aversion measure using a payoff outcome variable, necessarily leads to smaller estimated magnitudes and larger estimated slopes and elasticities for relative risk aversion.

This case of a constant W_0 is the easiest one to analyze, but also the least likely to be encountered. It is useful, however, in examining the effect of excluding components of wealth that are not constant, but are themselves random. As before, considering W_0 to be random complicates the analysis. Only the extreme case of W_0 distributed independently from X is discussed. In the research reviewed, the case of independence is encountered most often.

When W_0 is random and distributed independently from X, the equation $v(X) = E_{W_0} u(W - W_0)$ provides the relationship between the two utility functions $v(X)$ and $u(W)$. Using the same methodology as employed in Section 3.2 based on Pratt's (1964) analysis of convex combinations of utility functions, one can show that the relative risk aversion measures for $v(X)$, $R_v(X)$, is smaller than $R_u(W)$. It is again the case that the more inclusive outcome variable which is now W, has a larger magnitude of relative risk aversion than does outcome variable X. As before, even though W_0 is assumed to be random, since W_0 is positive, the relative risk aversion measure for $u(W)$ is larger than that for $v(X)$.

It can also be shown that the relative risk aversion measure for $v(X)$ tends to have a larger slope and elasticity than that for $u(W)$. Thus, the same broad conclusion that can drawn when W_0 is fixed also applies when W_0 is random and distributed independently from X. Focusing on payoff X and omitting components of wealth W, implies that the relative risk aversion measure that is obtained for outcome variable X is smaller than that for W, and has a slope and elasticity that tend to be larger. As observed earlier, the precise magnitude of these impacts cannot easily be determined unless W_0 is fixed.

In summary, when components of A-P wealth W, consumption C, or net income Y are omitted in order to focus on outcomes variable X which presents the payoff in a lottery, the measure of relative risk aversion that is determined from the decision maker's choices, $R_v(X)$, has a smaller measure of relative risk aversion and tends to be more positively sloped with a larger elasticity than does the relative risk aversion measure for W, C or Y, the outcome variable to which the payoff X is added.

6.2   Risk aversion when components are omitted

Many of the empirical studies reviewed in this section involve the analysis of choices made in an experimental settings or choices made in television game show settings. The outcome variable is referred to as a payoff and denoted X. Much of the discussion interpreting the findings that are reported involves determining which outcome variable the payoff X is added to, or equivalently, which outcome variable with significant omitted components is this payoff variable X equivalent to.

Levy (1994) conducts an experiment where first year MBA students make a series of portfolio decisions involving large sums of money, approximately USD30,000, and the payoff they receive for participating in the experiment is 1% of the outcome attained. He reports that the payoffs earned by the approximately sixty subjects range from USD33 to USD543 with an average payoff of USD70. For this payoff outcome variable, Levy finds strong evidence of decreasing absolute risk aversion, and also support for decreasing relative risk aversion for the average subject. Levy also has data concerning the subject's wealth outside the payoff from the experiment. On average this W_0 is USD35,641 so it is a substantial omitted component. Levy finds no evidence the level of relative risk aversion exhibited for payoff X is related to the size of W_0. He indicates that this may be due to framing or in the terminology used here, the payoff X and wealth W may not be part of the same choice set.

Another interpretation for the lack of effect of W_0 on the relative risk aversion for X is that in the mind of the subject, the payoff X is added to consumption rather than wealth. That is, the size of the payoffs are such that the subjects intend to use the payoff for current consumption rather than to allocate the payoff earned across many time periods. The evidence discussed in Section 4 indicates that relative risk aversion for consumption is likely to be large in magnitude and can be severely declining. Thus, if this payoff X is added to C rather than W, such an interpretation would imply that Levy's (1994) finding is consistent with other evidence concerning relative risk aversion for consumption.

Carlsson et al. (2005) (CDS) run two different experiments, one examining the risk aversion of the subject and the other dealing with inequality aversion. A total of 324 undergraduate students voluntarily participated in the experiment, and received no remuneration. Respondents make choices from a given set of lotteries. The N-M utility function used in making these choices was assumed to be constant relative risk averse with the outcome variable being the hypothetical payoff from the lottery chosen. No other form of wealth was mentioned or included in the analysis of the data. CDS find that the median magnitude of relative risk aversion is between 2 and 3. 63% of respondents display a relative risk aversion level for this payoff variable between 1 and 5, with the remainder falling outside that range.

Holt and Laury (2002) conduct a series of experiments where subjects choose among lotteries with a wide range of payoffs. Some of the payoffs were real and some were hypothetical, and range from several dollars to several hundred dollars. One question that is examined is whether or not risk aversion changes as the levels of the payoffs in the lottery are increased. Holt and Laury find that the majority of subjects are risk averse, even when payoff levels are low. The estimated magnitude of relative risk aversion, assuming a constant relative risk averse

N-M utility function, is 0.3 to 0.5 for relatively low payoffs, and 0.5 to 0.8 when the payoffs are increased by a factor of twenty. This increased relative risk aversion as the size of the payoff increases is consistent with the general discussion in Section 6.1. As X is a larger component of the general outcome variable, the relative risk aversion for X increases. Holt and Laury also use Saha's flexible power-expo utility function, and find that the typical subject exhibits increasing relative risk aversion and decreasing absolute risk aversion for this payoff outcome variable.

The decisions of game show participants have been extensively analyzed to determine the participant's risk taking propensities. A recent Wall Street Journal article Forelle (2006) discusses the game show "Deal or no Deal", where contestants choose one of twenty-six briefcases containing a random payoff between USD0.01 and USD1 million dollars. The twenty-five briefcases that are not selected are then opened a few at a time, revealing some information concerning the contents of the briefcase actually selected. At various stages in this process, the contestant is offered the chance to accept a fixed payoff rather than the unknown contents of the selected briefcase. These decisions can be used to provide information concerning the risk preferences of the contestant.

Fullenkamp et al. (2003) (FTB) use data from the television game show "Hossier Millionaire" to investigate risk preferences in a high-stakes environment. They find behavior to be largely characterized by risk aversion and the level of risk aversion varies directly with the size of the stakes involved in the gamble. This is consistent with the discussion in Section 6.1. The authors specify both a constant absolute and a constant relative risk averse form for the utility function, and estimate the parameters in the various utility specifications. Average values for absolute risk aversion range from 0.000048 to 0.000097. When assuming constant relative risk aversion, the estimated magnitude of relative risk aversion ranges from 0.64 to 1.43. FTB note that these estimates are smaller than those found in several other game show studies. FTB use payoffs rather than A-P wealth as the outcome variable because of the lack of other information concerning other components of wealth. These numbers are consistent with the payoff being added to the individual's A-P wealth, but being less than half of total wealth.

Beetsma and Schotman (2001) analyze behavior of players on the game show "Lingo" shown on Dutch television. Two appealing features of their study and data set are the large size of the payoffs, and a large sample size of decisions and individuals. The participants are assumed to maximize expected utility from the payoff. Non-game show wealth was not observed. Evidence of risk aversion is found, and using median values for Dutch household wealth to convert absolute risk aversion levels to magnitudes of relative risk aversion, estimates between 6 and 7 are obtained.

Other researchers have found evidence of very low risk aversion or near risk neutrality in game show environments. Hersch and McDougall (1997) use data from "Illinois Instant Riches" and assume a constant absolute risk averse utility function defined over payoff. They report that the estimated magnitude of absolute risk aversion is not significantly different from zero. Even with other formulations for the utility function, risk neutrality could not be rejected. Metrick (1995) uses data from the television game show "Jeopardy", and also finds that behavior is characterized by very low levels of risk aversion. These findings are all consistent with the observation that when outcome variable is a payoff which is only a small component of wealth, that very low levels of risk aversion are to be expected. It may also be the case that participants in game shows tend to less risk averse than the typical decison maker.

7

Summary and Conclusions

The stated purpose of this survey is to summarize, discuss, and interpret published research concerning the risk aversion of decision makers who maximize expected utility. In doing this, two points concerning measures of risk aversion are emphasized, and one broad conclusion is drawn from examining the research of the past forty years.

The first point receiving considerable emphasis is that any measure of risk aversion for a decision maker is specific to the particular outcome variable over which the measure is defined or estimated. Even small changes when defining or measuring an outcome variable can significantly alter the risk aversion function representing the decision maker's risk preferences. All statements concerning the magnitude, slope, or any other property of a risk aversion measure must implicitly or explicitly identify the outcome variable to which the statement applies. The profession has not fully recognized this point and considerable confusion concerning what is known about risk preferences is the result.

The second point of emphasis complements the first. Even when outcome variables differ, they are often related and if so, the relationship between outcome variables or their utility functions determines how their risk aversion measures differ. Such information also allows the risk aversion measure for one outcome variable to be adjusted or transformed into the risk aversion measure for the other. Relationships between outcome variables or their utility functions come from the definitions of the variables, from relationships established in economic models, and other sources.

These two relatively straightforward observations concerning risk aversion measures, allow the following broad conclusion to be drawn. A substantial portion of reported differences in magnitudes and slopes of risk aversion measures results from differences in the outcome variables that those risk aversion measures apply to. When the variation due to differences outcome variables is eliminated, the findings of the past forty years concerning measures of risk aversion are quite consistent. Contributions from economic theory and from empirical analysis for investors, consumers, or agricultural producers are more similar than casual reading would indicate.

Outcome variables differ from one another in at least two broad ways. First, for any particular outcome variable, by choosing which components to include, the variable can be defined or measured narrowly or broadly. In general, the more broadly an outcome variable is defined or measured, the larger the magnitude and the smaller the slope of its relative risk aversion measure. This type of difference in outcome variables explains much of disparity between the findings from economic theory and from empirical analysis. Theory tends to use narrow definitions, while broader measures tend to be used in empirical analysis.

The second way in which outcome variables differ involves the distinction between stock and flow variables. Flow outcome variables such as consumption and income or profit, tend to have relative risk aversion measures with a larger magnitude and smaller slope than does a stock variable such as wealth. Gollier (2002) explains this using the term "time diversification" indicating that for a stock variable like wealth the risk associated with it can be "shared with one's future selves". As a consequence avoiding risk for this outcome variable is less important to the decision maker.

In the Epilogue of his recent book, Christian Gollier (2001) says that

It is quite surprising and disappointing to me that almost 40 years after the establishment of the concept of risk aversion by Pratt and Arrow, our profession has not been able to attain a consensus about the measurement of risk aversion.

While we agree with this statement, we do add the comment that there is more of a consensus than casual inspection of the evidence indicates.

References

Arrow, K. (1965), *Aspects of the Theory of Risk Bearing.* Helsinki: Yrjo Jahnssonin Saatio.

Arrow, K. (1971), *Essays in the Theory of Risk Bearing.* New York: Markham.

Bajtelsmit, V. L., A. Bernasek, and N. A. Jianaloplos (1999), 'Gender differences in defined contribution pension decisions'. *Financial Services Review* **8**, 1–10.

Baron, D. P. (1970), 'Price uncertainty, utility, and industry equilibrium in pure competition'. *International Economic Review* **11**(3), 463–480.

Barsky, R. B., F. T. Juster, M. S. Kimball, and M. D. Shapiro (1997), 'Preference parameters and behavioral heterogeneity: An experimental approach in the health and retirement study'. *Quarterly Journal of Economics* **112**(2), 537–579.

Beetsma, R. M. W. J. and P. C. Schotman (2001), 'Measuring risk attitudes in a natural experiment: Data from the television game show lingo'. *The Economic Journal* **111**(474), 821–848.

Bellante, D. and C. A. Green (2004), 'Relative risk aversion among the elderly'. *Review of Financial Economics* **13**(3), 269–281.

Bellante, D. and R. P. Saba (1986), 'Human capital and life-cycle effects on risk aversion'. *The Journal of Financial Research* **9**(1), 41–52.

Blake, D. (1996), 'Efficiency, risk aversion and portfolio insurance: An analysis of financial asset portfolios held by investors in the United Kingdom'. *The Economic Journal* **106**(438), 1175–1192.

Bontems, P. and A. Thomas (2000), 'Information value and risk premium in agricultural production: The case of split nitrogen application for corn'. *American Journal of Agricultural Economics* **82**(1), 59–70.

Briys, E., G. Dionne, and L. Eeckhoudt (1989), 'More on insurance as a giffen good'. *Journal of Risk and Uncertainty* **2**(4), 415–420.

Briys, E. and L. Eeckhoudt (1985), 'Relative risk aversion in comparative statics: Comment'. *American Economic Review* **75**(1), 281–283.

Carlsson, F., D. Daruvala, and O. Johansson-Stenman (2005), 'Are people inequality-averse or just risk-averse?'. *Economica* **72**(287), 375–396.

Cass, D. and J. E. Stiglitz (1972), 'Risk aversion and wealth effects on portfolios with many assets'. *The Review of Economic Studies* **39**(3), 331–354.

Chavas, J.-P. and M. T. Holt (1996), 'Economic behavior under uncertainty: A joint analysis of risk preferences and technology'. *Review of Economics and Statistics* **78**(2), 329–335.

Cohn, R. A., W. G. Lewellen, R. C. Lease, and G. G. Schlarbaum (1975), 'Individual investor risk aversion and investment portfolio composition'. *Journal of Finance* **30**(2), 605–620.

Constantinides, G. M. (1990), 'Habit formation: A resolution of the equity premium puzzle'. *Journal of Political Economy* **98**(3), 519–543.

Dalal, A. J. and B. G. Arshanapalli (1993), 'Estimating the demand for risky assets via the indirect expected utility function'. *Journal of Risk and Uncertainty* **6**(3), 277–288.

Demers, F. and M. Demers (1991), 'Increases in risk and othe optimal deductible'. *Journal of Risk and Insurance* **58**(4), 670–699.

Diamond, P. A. and J. E. Stiglitz (1974), 'Increases in risk and in risk aversion'. *Journal of Economic Theory* **8**(3), 337–360.

Eeckhoudt, L. and C. Gollier (1995), *Risk: Evaluation, Management and Sharing*. New York: Harvester Wheatsheaf, first edition. First published in french in 1992, translated by Val Lambson into english in 1995.

Eeckhoudt, L., C. Gollier, and H. Schlesinger (1996), 'Changes in background risk and risk taking behavior'. *Econometrica* **64**(3), 683–689.

Eeckhoudt, L., C. Gollier, and H. Schlesinger (2005), *Economic and Financial Decisions Under Risk*. Princeton, New Jersey: Princeton University Press.

Eeckhoudt, L. and M. Kimball (1992), 'Background risk, prudence, and the demand for insurance'. In: G. Dionne (ed.): paper appeared in *Contributions to Insurance Economics*, Boston, pp. 239–254, Kluwer Academic Publishers.

Eeckhoudt, L., J. Meyer, and M. B. Ormiston (1997), 'The interaction between the demand for insurance and insurable assets'. *Journal of Risk and Uncertainty* **14**(1), 25–39.

Eeckhoudt, L. R. and J. K. Hammitt (2001), 'Background risks and the value of a statistical life'. *Journal of Risk and Uncertainty* **23**(3), 261–279.

Eichner, T. and A. Wagener (2004), 'Relative risk aversion, relative prudence and comparative statics under uncertainty: The case of (mu, sigma)-preferences'. *Bulletin of Economic Research* **56**(2), 159–170.

Eichner, T. and A. Wagener (2005), 'Measures of risk attiitude: Correspondences between mean-variance and expected utility approaches'. *Decisions in Economics and Finance* **28**(1), 53–65.

Fishburn, P. C. and R. B. Porter (1976), 'Optimal portfolios with one safe and one risky asset: Effects of changes in rate of return and risk'. *Management Science* **22**(10), 1064–1073.

Forelle, C. (2006), 'Why game shows have economists glued to their TVs'. Article in Wall Street Journal; January 12, 2006; page A1. staff reporter for Wall Street Journal.

Friedman, M. and L. J. Savage (1948), 'The utility analysis of choices involving risk'. *Journal of Political Economy* **56**(4), 279–304.

Friedman, M. and L. J. Savage (1952), 'The expected utility hypothesis and the measurability of utility'. *Journal of Political Economy* **60**(6), 463–474.

Friend, I. and M. E. Blume (1975), 'The demand for risky assets'. *American Economic Review* **65**(5), 900–922.

Fullenkamp, C., R. Tonorio, and R. Battalio (2003), 'Assessing individual risk attitudes using field data from lottery games'. *Review of Economics and Statistics* **85**(1), 218–226.

Gollier, C. (2001), *The Economics of Risk and Time*. Cambridge, MA: The MIT Press.

Gollier, C. (2002), 'Time diversification, liquidity constraints, and decreasing aversion to risk on wealth'. *Journal of Monetary Economics* **49**, 1439–1459.

Gollier, C. and J. W. Pratt (1996), 'Risk vulnerability and the tempering effect of background risk'. *Econometrica* **64**, 1109–1123.

Hadar, J. and T. K. Seo (1990), 'The effects of shifts in a return distribution on optimal portfolios'. *International Economic Review* **31**(3), 721–736.

Hadar, J. and T. K. Seo (1993), 'Sensible risk aversion'. Department of Economics, Southern Methodist University.

Halek, M. and J. G. Eisenhauer (2001), 'Demography of risk aversion'. *Journal of Risk and Insurance* **68**(1), 1–24.

Hersch, P. L. and G. S. McDougall (1997), 'Decison making under uncertainty when the stakes are high: Evidence from a lottery game show'. *Southern Economic Journal* **64**(1), 75–84.

Hey, J. D. (1985), 'Relative risk aversion in comparative statics: Comment'. *American Economic Review* **75**(1), 284–285.

Hirshleifer, J. and J. G. Riley (1992), *The Analytics of Uncertainty and Information*, Surveys of Economic Literature. New York: Cambridge, first edition.

Holt, C. and S. Laury (2002), 'Risk aversion and incentive effects'. *American Economic Review* **92**(5), 1644–1655.

Ichiishi, T. (1997), *Microeconomic Theory*. Cambridge, Mass.: Blackwell Publishers, first edition.

Jianakoplos, N. A. and A. Bernasek (1998), 'Are women more risk averse?'. *Economic Inquiry* **36**(4), 620–630.

Kaplow, L. (2005), 'The value of statistical life and the coefficient of relative risk aversion'. *Journal of Risk and Uncertainty* **31**(1), 23–34.

Katz, E. (1983), 'Relative risk aversion in comparative statics'. *American Economic Review* **73**(3), 452–453.

Kihlstrom, R. E., D. Romer, and S. Williams (1981), 'Risk aversion with random initial wealth'. *Econometrica* **49**(4), 911–920.

Kimball, M. S. (1993), 'Standard risk aversion'. *Econometrica* **61**, 589–611.

Kimball, M. S. and N. G. Mankiw (1989), 'Precautionary saving and the timing of taxes'. *Journal of Political Economy* **97**(4), 863–879.

Kumbhakar, S. C. (2002), 'Specification and estimation of production risk, risk preferences and technical efficiency'. *American Journal of Agricultural Economics* **84**(1), 8–22.

Leland, H. E. (1968), 'Saving and uncertainty: The precautionary demand for saving'. *Quarterly Journal of Economics* **82**(3), 465–473.

Lence, S. H. (2000), 'Using consumption and asset return data to estimate farmers' time preferences and risk attitudes'. *American Journal of Agricultural Economics* **82**(4), 934–947.

Levy, H. (1994), 'Absolute and relative risk aversion: An experimental study'. *Journal of Risk and Uncertainty* **8**(3), 289–307.

Löffler, A. (2001), 'A μ-σ-risk aversion paradox and wealth dependent utility'. *Journal of Risk and Uncertainty* **23**(1), 57–73.

Menezes, C. F. and D. L. Hanson (1970), 'On the theory of risk aversion'. *International Economic Review* **11**(3), 481–487.

Metrick, A. (1995), 'A natural experiment in "jeopardy"'. *American Economic Review* **85**(1), 240–253.

Meyer, D. J. and J. Meyer (1998), 'Changes in background risk and the demand for insurance'. *The Geneva Papers on Risk and Insurance Theory* **23**(1), 29–40.

Meyer, D. J. and J. Meyer (1999), 'The comparative statics of deductible insurance and insurable assets'. *Journal of Risk and Insurance* **66**(1), 1–15.

Meyer, D. J. and J. Meyer (2005a), 'Risk preferences in multi-period consumption models, the equity premium puzzle, and habit formation utility'. *Journal of Monetary Economics* **52**(8), 1497–1515.

Meyer, D. J. and J. Meyer (2005b), 'Relative risk aversion: What do we know?'. *Journal of Risk and Uncertainty* **31**(3), 243–262.

Meyer, J. (1987), 'Two-moment decision models and expected utility maximization'. *American Economic Review* **77**(3), 421–430.

Meyer, J. and M. B. Ormiston (1994), 'The effect of optimal portfolios of changing the return to a risky asset: The case of dependent risky returns'. *International Economic Review* **35**(3), 603–612.

Mitchell, D. W. (1994), 'Relative risk aversion with arrow-debreu securities'. *International Economic Review* **35**(1), 257–258.

Morin, R.-A. and A. F. Suarez (1983), 'Risk aversion revisited'. *The Journal of Finance* **38**(4), 1201–1216.

Mossin, J. (1968), 'Aspects of rational insurance purchasing'. *Journal of Political Economy* **76**(4, Part 1), 553–568.

Nachman, D. C. (1982), 'Preservation of "More Risk Averse" under expectations'. *Journal of Economic Theory* **28**(2), 361–368.

Ogaki, M. and Q. Zhang (2001), 'Decreasing relative risk aversion and tests of risk sharing'. *Econometrica* **69**(2), 515–526.

Pratt, J. W. (1964), 'Risk aversion in the small and in the large'. *Econometrica* **32**(1–2), 83–98.

Riley, W. B. and K. V. Chow (1992), 'Asset allocation and individual risk aversion'. *Financial Analysts Journal* **48**(6), 32–37.

Roche, M. (2005), 'The equity premium puzzle and decreasing relative risk aversion'. The National University of Ireland, Maynooth. Forthcoming in Applied Financial Economics Letters.

Rothchild, M. and J. E. Stiglitz (1971), 'Inceasing risk II: Its economic consequences'. *Journal of Economic Theory* **3**(1), 66–84.

Rubinstein, A. (2006), *Lecture Notes in Microeconomic Theory*. Princeton, NJ: Princeton University Press.

Saha, A. (1997), 'Risk preference estitmation in the nonlinear mean standard deviation approach'. *Economic Inquiry* **35**(4), 770–782.

Saha, A., C. R. Shumway, and H. Talpaz (1994), 'Joint estimation of risk preference structure and technology using expo-power utility'. *American Journal of Agricultural Economics* **76**(2), 173–184.

Sandmo, A. (1968), 'Portfolio choice in a theory of saving'. *Swedish Journal of Economics* **70**(2), 106–122.

Sandmo, A. (1970), 'The effect of uncertainty on saving decisions'. *The Review of Economic Studies* **37**(3), 353–360.

Sandmo, A. (1971), 'On the theory of the competitive firm under price uncertainty'. *American Economic Review* **61**(1), 65–73.

Schlesinger, H. (1981), 'The optimal level of deductibility in insurance contracts'. *Journal of Risk and Insurance* **48**(3), 465–481.

Schooley, D. K. and D. D. Worden (1996), 'Risk aversion measures: Comparing attitudes and asset allocation'. *Financial Services Review* **5**(2), 87–99.

Sunden, A. E. and B. J. Surette (1998), 'Gender differences in the allocation of assets in retirement savings plans'. *American Economic Review* **88**(2), 207–211.

Viscusi, W. K. and J. E. Aldy (2003), 'The value of statistical life: A critical review of market estimates throughout the World'. *Journal of Risk and Uncertainty* **27**(1), 5–76.

Von Neumann, J. and O. Morgenstern (1944), *Theory of Games and Economic Behavior*. Princeton, New Jersey: Princeton University Press.

Wang, H. and S. Hanna (1997), 'Does risk tolerance decrease with age'. *Financial Counseling and Planning* **8**(2), 27–31.

Wilson, R. (1968), 'The theory of syndicates'. *Econometrica* **36**(1), 119–132.

Zeckhauser, R. and E. Keeler (1970), 'Another type of risk aversion'. *Econometrica* **38**(5), 661–665.

CPSIA information can be obtained at www.ICGtesting.com
Printed in the USA
BVOW011133231212

308908BV00002B/53/A